HEGEL'S TRANSCENDENTAL INDUCTION

Peter Simpson

STATE UNIVERSITY OF NEW YORK PRESS

Published by
State University of New York Press, Albany

Printed in the United States of America

For information, address State University of New York Press,
State University Plaza, Albany, N.Y., 12246

Production by Cathleen Collins
Marketing by Anne Valentine

Library of Congress Cataloging in Publication Data

Simpson, Peter, 1961–
Hegel's transcendental induction / Peter Simpson.
p. cm. — (SUNY series in Hegelian studies)
Includes bibliographical references and index.
ISBN 0–7914–3275–0. — ISBN 0–7914–3276–9 (pbk.)
1. Hegel, Georg Wilhelm Friedrick, 1770–1830—Contribution in logic. 2. Induction (Logic) I. Title. II. Series.
B2949.L8S55 1996
193—dc20 96–22520
CIP

10 9 8 7 6 5 4 3 2 1

Contents

HEGEL'S TRANSCENDENTAL INDUCTION

SUNY Series in Hegelian Studies
Edited by William Desmond

Introduction

> The whole of the Idea in itself is science as perfected and complete: but on the other side is the beginning, the process of its origination. This process of the origination of science is different from its process in itself when it is complete, just as is the process of the history of Philosophy and that of Philosophy itself.
>
> —Hegel, *Lectures on the History of Philosophy*

Hegel's *Phenomenology of Spirit* claims to offer the reader the opportunity to participate in the "process of origination," the "coming-to-be of Science as such or of knowledge."[1] Indeed, the argument in the text proceeds in response to the demand, made by the individual who takes seriously the claims made by science to have comprehended the truth of experience—that science show the individual how to develop the scientific standpoint from its experience. This responsiveness on the part of science marks the *Phenomenology of Spirit*, I will argue, as a text that proceeds, from the perspective of the development of a scientific comprehension, inductively.

Notice two things about the kind of argument I am going to undertake in this reading of the *Phenomenology of Spirit*: first, that it does not challenge the legitimacy of describing the text as deductive, a claim advanced by Hegel himself in his *Science of Logic*,[2] and developed with careful attention to detail by a number of commentators;[3] and second, that in recognizing the inductive origination of the concept of science, or experience, one is not "translating" Hegel's project into the highly determinate conceptual vocabulary of so-called analytic philosophy, but rather respecting the significance of the "process of origination."[4] Let me briefly speak about these two issues before looking at ways in which Hegel himself, without using the term *induction*, flags the originary process within his text.

That Hegel's text has been constructed scientifically is a feature of its argument, made explicit at a number of points. As I have already suggested, it recounts not a process of discovery but a response to the demand for a kind of scientific education, a demand Hegel describes as legitimately made of the scientist.[5] If the response is to lead the student to science, it cannot proceed haphazardly, but must be already "scientific"—that is, the work of science, the way it understands and comprehends as necessary the requisite developmental stages that will culminate in a scientific understanding. In this sense, science must deduce from its own conceptual self-understanding these necessary stages, stages that then will be held together by a formal and rigorous logic.

But if what has been at stake in response to the demand of the individual is to some extent the individual's reluctance to recognize the truth of the scientific (and "inverted") standpoint, with its talk of method, necessity, and universality, then science will win only part of the battle by demonstrating its self-closure in deductive terms: the individual will still be in a position to say that science can show why we must end up as scientists, only by a kind of question-begging. What if I don't grant the science of experience its first premises, or the necessity that its conceptual rigor expresses? In other words, must I not already be a scientist to perform such a deduction, and doesn't it therefore leave me with the truths I know I have in my experiencing, outside?

This is a very serious question, for Hegel and for science, and it is clearly the source of a tradition of challenging Hegel's claims—from Kierkegaard to Foucault the charge is raised again and again that scientific closure begs the vital experiential questions. But Hegel's argument in the *Phenomenology of Spirit* does more than respond to the concerned or skeptical individual: Hegel's argument insists that this individual mark the origin of science, that it be the individual's concern, in conjunction with the ultimacy of scientific self-closure, which incites and measures the completeness of science.

But this is more than the rather commonplace observation that "things look different on the way up than they do on the way down." They are, as the text cited at the outset of this introduction suggests, different processes, reconcilable perhaps, but distinct. To open science up to the demand that its presentation find a (seemingly) nonscientific point of departure (or, from the standpoint of deducing an educational program, point of culmination) is a revolution in the very concept of science. This revolution is described by Hegel in different ways in different texts, often as a criticism of what he calls "formalism," but in every case the claim is made that science cannot posit or announce, from within its own methodology, its self-closure. It must instead articulate the self-determining self-closure of the matter itself. It is in this sense that there is an inductive argument, and an argument about induction, in the *Phenomenology of Spirit*.

Hegel's responses to Kant have long been the subject of scholarly debate, but if there is anything like consensus in that debate, it centers around the positing of a concept of experience from which Kant derives his transcendental deduction.[6] It is a distinctive feature of Kant's argument that whatever the transcendental features of consciousness yield us in experiencing we must be able to describe them as self-closing or internally necessary if we are to use them to make knowledge claims. Kant's argument, which rests in large measure on his experience of reading Hume, suggests that self-legislating reason makes universal and necessary claims and that these are the stuff of knowledge, so questions about the ways in which these reflective judgements admit of 'otherness' are literally beside the point; they are necessary, objective, and rational, and that is what we want our science, or knowledge, to be.

As I have described it, the concept of science we find developed in the *Phenomenology of Spirit* replies in at least two ways to Kant. The first of these is to ask, as Hegel does in the introduction to his work, whether this has not precisely abandoned the goals of knowing in order to provide a kind of security or certainty, a certainty that would have to be ultimately discouraging if one were certain that one had conceded the very project one was engaged in to claim one had succeeded at it. The second reply might pick up on the discussion, in Kant's preface, of the "timeliness" of his work and its usefulness in responding to a contemporary malaise in thinking philosophically. If his work is essentially motivated by the need to respond to a prevailing skepticism or indifference, then even its strict positivism is itself already driven by a kind of experiencing to respond in a positivistic fashion. Kant would have already sacrificed the ideal of a timeless epistemology or metaphysics in arguing that *now* is the time for such a philosophy.

The change in the concept of science accomplished in the *Phenomenology of Spirit* takes place along the two lines of criticism just mentioned. On the one hand, Hegel will argue that a wholly positivistic response to the challenge of making sense of our experience subverts the challenge, and so cannot ever count as its completion; on the other hand, any such response is already the result of our being affected by our experience of trying to make sense of the world, thus a tacit refusal of positivism.

As Hegel describes the process in his introduction, experiencing itself decides the fate of the ways we attempt to organize and make sense of it. It is in and as experiencing that the various strategies are formulated, advanced, and evaluated. When science takes seriously the demands of the individual then it cannot reply with the suggestion that if only one were able to see the brilliant success of a mathematical model of cognition one would adopt it enthusiastically. Rather, it must show the individual that the individual's own experiencing demands that it be comprehended scientifically: it must show, in other words, that the science of experience is literally *of* experiencing itself and not the unilateral construction that follows from scientific models, methods, or assumptions.

It is in this sense then that the concept of experience develops inductively toward scientific comprehension, and is presented deductively as the inductive process it must have been, for the education of the individual. If the criterion is, in every case, experiencing itself, then the individual must learn from experience how it demands to be comprehended. Notice that this argument makes the discussion of Hegel's method a curious compromise of the text's argument: taken literally, or according to its own prescriptions, Hegel's science of experiencing can have no method other than what experience provides for itself.[7] If the scientist prepares for the student of experience a "ladder to the Absolute," it must be a ladder constructed in accordance with the experientially generated method it has comprehended.

My goal, in this work, is to describe how the development of the *Phenomenology of Spirit* depends both on experience, or arises from experience inductively, and on the individual who aspires to scientific comprehension and who must learn to become more responsive to, and less positivistic toward, experiencing. In other words, I will argue that the development is both inductive as a whole and *about* becoming inductive: it is an argument that concludes with the concept of the inductive science it has described only if we come to share the inductive responsiveness that has made the argument possible.[8] Or, in the language I will use in making my argument, a process that is inductive *in-itself* culminates in our becoming inductive *in- and for-ourselves.*

Induction is not a word Hegel uses to describe his scientific project, but he provides us with a number of ways of imaging that project that are at least suggestive of induction.[9] Three helpful examples include: education, history, and experience itself. I have already discussed the importance of the education metaphor, but again let me briefly pursue it.

The goal of education is to lead someone into a deeper or richer understanding. Indeed, this leading in is already a helpful parallel with induction. But notice how education works: One is typically required to perform a set of determinate tasks; then, on the basis of having mastered the skills involved, one is able to move to a "higher" set of tasks, with the same pattern of task-performance-transformed-task repeating itself as the student works toward comprehension of the subject matter.[10] It is crucial to the process of education that certain tasks depend on our becoming experienced with others and that some reflection on what experiencing offers leads us forward.

"History" is another term Hegel uses to describe the argument in the *Phenomenology of Spirit*, a term he employs in ways that stretch its usage in the more familiar context of his lecture courses on history. The argument here is the "detailed history of the *education* of consciousness itself to the standpoint of Science,"[11] and so again there is some manner of reflection about the ways in which experiencing has shaped the notion or concept of experience. It is a commonplace to attribute to Hegel the becoming-historical of knowing, but it seems widely overlooked that the problems of a historical epistemology—how it comprehends what has happened and how it justifies its comprehension—are very much associated with inductive epistemology, which is again typically understood to be an inference made on the basis of a range of completed experience.

Finally, the concept of experience itself suggests an inductive element, as it must have for those who read Hegel's work in the milieu of early modern philosophical debates about knowledge and science. Hegel has clearly sided with Kant and the skeptical tradition in making experience a philosophical concern, yet, as I have suggested, challenged the philosophical privilege that would decide on experience's behalf how we are prepared to let it occur.[12] If our science takes its cue from experience, if it is to let experience reveal to us its inner unity, then we are, in the tradition of Bacon (the figure in question in the citation that opened this introduction), inductive scientists.

Three terms—education, history, and experience—roughly form the contexts for the third, fourth, and fifth chapters of this work. In the first chapter, I describe the experience of sensuous certainty and its transition into perception in terms of induction. Following a rather lengthy excursus that addresses the legitimacy of this term, I show how perception has arisen through an implicit confrontation with experiencing and that it is through our attempt to win the immediacy promised by sensuous certainty that we are able to see the experientially mediated origin of perception.

The second chapter pursues two attempts to gather together the loose threads of perceptual experiencing and tie them together in a posited unity of experiencing. The first of these, understanding consciousness, claims to be comprehensive in its knowing, but its exclusion of the moment of difference or diversity reveals the need for comprehension to respect the self-differentiating nature of experiencing. With desiring self-consciousness, the second of the two, we move to those forms of knowledge that take the activity of selfhood as the unifying ground of experiencing. It is through this experience that we learn why we must become inductive: that is, why the positing of an immediate unity literally threatens to destroy the project of making sense of the world.

Chapter 3 focuses on the experience of slavery. There are three levels on which the analysis proceeds, but central to all three is what I call the slave's inductive approach to its work. It is, I argue, just because the slave is responsive to the demands of its experienced otherness, or prepared to learn from experience how it demands to be treated, that it is able to satisfy the master's demands and develop a sense of itself.

But the slave is unable to develop fully the fruits of its inductive labor because of the institution of slavery, the way in which its labor is consumed without being recognized as the work of the self, and because it has not yet developed an appropriately scientific sense of what belongs to it as experiencing. These two dimensions of slavery, institutional life and conceptual unity, remain concealed.

In the fourth chapter, I follow the institutional development of social life as it works to effect the kind of recognition absent in slavery. Within the broader context of institutional life, the need to adopt an inductive attitude toward self-discovery is coupled with the need for an institutional sanction for such a model of the citizen or member. My argument details the history of institutional life in these terms. It is only in a conscientious community, I argue, and one that understands conscience in terms of forgiveness that inductive selfhood becomes an explicit and sanctioned objective. In my concluding chapter, I trace this realization of induction into Hegel's chapter on Absolute Knowing and show how phenomenology is induction in- and for-itself.

While my argument as a whole seems to challenge the conventional wisdom regarding Hegelian philosophy, it is certainly not alone in making the kind of argument it does. A number of scholars have pursued similar themes, and their work has played, in some cases, an important role in my own. John Sallis and Jay Lampert, for example, have argued in different ways for a model of Hegelian science that encompasses the themes of self-determining content and experiential "bias" that has helped me understand how Hegel argues.[13]

More explicitly "empirical" is George Schrader's compact "Hegel's Contribution to Phenomenology," which bucks several trends in phenomenology at once. Foremost among these, for my purposes here, is his argument that Hegel is (what Hegel might call) the conscience of phenomenology, the phenomenologist who saw most clearly and expressed most vehemently the empiricism at the core of phenomenological analysis. For Schrader, it is precisely because of its diligence in respecting the ways experience is expressive of itself that phenomenology gains a purchase on the history of philosophy, and, he argues, none have taken this more seriously, more *empirically*, than Hegel.

But the most important scholar from the perspective of my work is John Russon, in two ways. First, as a teacher, Russon insists on taking Hegel seriously, reading his works as if it were possible they might deliver what they promise. His refusal to accept or repeat the dismissive prejudices, many of which come from Hegel scholars, which would suggest Hegel dreamed of more than ever worked itself out in his philosophy, and required his students to read the text carefully with a keenness for argument.

It is in his published (and unpublished)[14] work that Russon's originality as a thinker and his influence on my work is most clear. Several key stages of my own argument are shaped by ways in which Russon has read the *Phenomenology of Spirit*—the role of education in slavery, the primacy of conscientious forgiveness and its relation to phenomenology, for example— and this work develops an insight he made into the inductive or empiricist lessons of the analysis of the Unhappy Consciousness.[15]

A number of other philosophers have lent their support to this work, and I am extremely grateful to them. They include Kenneth L. Schmitz, my first Hegel teacher who supported this project by commenting on an earlier draft and by helping me to begin making sense of the *Science of Logic*; H. S. Harris, who also commented on an earlier draft and encouraged me to pursue its publication; Rebecca Comay, who read an earlier draft and made some important suggestions; John McCumber, who encouraged me in a similar manner; Graeme Nicholson, who challenged my reading vigorously at every stage and made it a better argument in the process; and Robert Bernasconi, who invited me to present part of this work to his graduate class, which was reading the *Phenomenology of Spirit*, and who has been a very supportive person throughout my career. Thanks also to William Desmond and two anonymous reviewers for the State University of New York Press, for their help and criticism, and the staff at SUNY Press, including Cathleen Collins, for their professionalism. To my family, Anne, Ruth, and Charlie, and to friends, especially John Russon, Patricia Fagan, David Morris, and Jay Lampert, thank you all for your encouragement and support.

CHAPTER ONE

The Experience of Conscious Life

Introduction

In this chapter, my goal is to describe the shape of consciousness Hegel calls *Wahrnehmen*, or perception, as *inductive in-itself*. That is, I will argue that the experience of perceptual consciousness depends on its being mediated by the experience of consciousness as such, despite its being unaware of the precise nature of its dependence. Specifically, perceptual consciousness depends on the experience of having to recognize that sensible details are aspects of a manifold. I will focus primarily on the way perception responds to its experience and its implications for our understanding of what the task is with which we emerge from the experience of perceptual consciousness.

Hegel's phenomenological analysis of sensuous certainty, the shape of conscious life which inaugurates the science of the experience of consciousness, has spurred a number of critical commentaries, each of which fastens in some way on an alleged contamination of the immediacy which Hegel claims is its defining feature as a shape of consciousness.[1] While I am concerned more, as I have mentioned, with the implications of the transition into perception than with the analysis of sensuous certainty alone, I take my reading of Hegel's analysis to show why any contamination of sensuous certainty must already be its own doing and why the only legitimate attempts to defend or preserve its immediacy are made by perception.

Sensuous Certainty

Sensuous certainty, the manner of experiencing that is best characterized by the phrase "there's nothing to it," presents a paradoxical beginning to the *Phenomenology of Spirit*. On the one hand, what we seem to learn is that it is not, and could not be, a way of experiencing at all. Of all the shapes of conscious life examined in the course of the argument, it is uniquely untenable: the very independence from mediation it proclaims precludes language, content, and meaning. Hegel's editorial remarks at the outset of the chapter devoted to sensuous certainty slide from a description of the necessity of immediacy for the beginning of our science, through a brief portrayal of sensuous certainty, to the outright repudiation of sensuous certainty as a form of knowledge.[2]

On the other hand, sensuous certainty is there as the beginning, and moreover as the one form of conscious life whose place we are supposed to accept as self-evidently necessary, or rather, the form we are to accept without imposing our own standards of unity or necessity. Of its placement, Hegel responds rather weakly that "our object cannot be anything else but immediate knowledge itself."[3]

The paradox, then, is that of a shape of consciousness explicitly denigrated while at the same time granted an immunity from the demands of conceptual thinking, of a form of conscious life that is both uniquely impracticable and uniquely necessitated.

One of the opening sections of Hegel's *Science of Logic*, entitled "With What Must the Science Begin?,"[4] helps somewhat in clarifying the situation regarding sensuous certainty, but equally carries with it the risk of conflating the very distinct concerns for beginnings appropriate to each text.[5] In what follows, I will attempt to bridge the remarks from Hegel's *Science of Logic* to the issues specific to sensuous certainty, using Hegel's scattered remarks on beginnings in the *Phenomenology of Spirit* as a backdrop.[6]

There are three claims made in the *Science of Logic* that have a bearing on the place of sensuous certainty: the inseparability of mediation and immediacy; the fact that immediacy is already a reflective determination, that is, mediated by its exclusion of mediation; and the argument that the immediacy of the beginning can only be comprehended in its necessity in light of the conclusion, in which mediation is revealed as the working of a self-mediating totality, hence immediate in the sense that it is unconditioned by any external forces.

The first of these claims seems to prompt the remark that the only suitable beginning is immediate knowledge. If there is no mediation without immediacy, and no immediacy without mediation, from the standpoint of the self-comprehension of experiencing immediate knowledge begs no questions, or rather begs them all, leaving the whole of the mediating that necessarily belongs to it to be exposed. The alternative, some mediated principle of cognition like the instrumental theory of knowledge described in the introduction to the *Phenomenology of Spirit*, would equally show itself to require further mediation because of the immediacy with which it is taken up as the beginning, but it would leave unexamined the development leading up to such a theory. Sensuous certainty is the paradigm of undeveloped experiencing, the form of experiencing which claims that no development is necessary or possible. It thereby poses the task of the complete course of development, which is the necessary object of science.[7]

At the same time, it is inherently problematic as a "primitive" form of conscious life, precisely because it must already be mediated by the exclusion of mediation. It is a reflective claim, a kind of extremist empiricism, and in this respect it could never be what it says it is—experiencing simpliciter. It is, rather, already a (crudely, and hence the disparaging remarks of Hegel's) philosophical reflection on experiencing.[8] The reflective relationship shows up in sensuous certainty as a claim made prior to experiencing which demonstrates in experiencing that it could only have been made by excluding conscious life altogether. In this respect, what we see in its experience is as much the refutation of crude or naive empiricism as it is the letting-be of the form of conscious life prescribed by the opening paragraph of the phenomenological argument. That we learn that experiencing as described by sensuous certainty is impossible, then, says as much about the reflective position it has adopted as it does about how experiencing occurs.[9]

The third claim, which is in fact one of the most profound conclusions we reach at the end of the text, concerns the continuity between the position sensuous certainty holds as a beginning and the culmination of the process it initiates. It is only when immediacy is shown to be the result of self-mediation, a mediated immediacy, that the necessity that experiencing show up as immediate is comprehended.[10] To be sure, the immediacy of self-mediation is a far cry from the impoverished content of sensuous certainty; but the objective, that experiencing speak for itself and be unconditioned by extraneous terms, is consistent with the goal of science, and the end, in effect, confirms the demand of the beginning.[11]

What makes compelling the placement of sensuous certainty at the inception of the argument is, in the end, the combination of the goal of immediacy, that what we experience is self-determining and not dependent on anything external, and the necessity that we recognize that immediacy does show itself to depend on mediation. That is, we can take nothing else as our beginning, because we cannot posit its dependence on anything but must experience its dependence as its self-mediation.

With the claim that there "is nothing" to knowing what is, the sense-certain consciousness presents us with the claim, not that the work of experiencing is already done, but that there is none to do. Sensuous certainty is the claim that experiencing simply is, or it simply happens. Putting this claim to work we learn that there is something to be done, if only to preserve the aspects of being sensuous certainty tries to claim for itself.

Sensuous certainty can claim to be immediate knowing precisely because it ostensibly recognizes nothing other than what is. It carries no expectations over and against the being of its objects and no standards other than its own openness to being, or its receptivity. Its immediacy lies in the autonomy of its objects, in their being unopposed or unrelated to any distinct cognitive elements through which they come to be. In Hegelian terms, nothing recognized by sensuous certainty is external to, and therefore mediating for, the truth of the content of its awareness. It is on the basis of this undifferentiated integrity of its experienced other that its claim to be the purest kind of knowing is supposed to be secured.

Even in its accounting for its immediacy, however, we can see that there are a number of distinctions present. As we watch it engage in being certain, these distinctions will show up as contradicting its claim of immediate knowledge. As Hegel notes, it is its own work that raises these ultimately terminal objections, and it is to its own work that we immediately turn.

Initially, like the other two forms of object-oriented conscious life that arise from its ashes, the individual who is certain of its sensory awareness takes this to be a claim about the way things are. That is, it distinguishes its certainty from its object, and introduces the dualism of what it is aware of and its own awareness. This is precisely the kind of distinction it ought not to have made, because its immediacy depends on not having to recognize (or not having to have already bridged) real distinctions. To admit them is precisely to admit mediation, a crisis that sensuous certainty initially hopes to avert by assigning first its object, and then the certain knower itself, ontological primacy.[12] What it will discover is that even taken singly, the terms through which it seeks to salvage its immediacy demand mediation.

In making its initial claim about what is, sensuous certainty focuses on that of which it is receptive and singles out something from this spatio-temporal field of awareness. This object, then, is the basis or ground of my certainty. It is because it is that I am certain of it.

On closer inspection, however, that of which it is certain has to speak for itself and provide its own determinateness. But if that determinacy involves, at the very least, distinguishing its object from its (unessential) certainty, it cannot be immediate, and the question arises, of what can it be certain? Sensuous certainty seeks to avoid any determination of its object that could be introduced from outside, and so its reply can only be in terms of the objective determining of its field: it is now, or it is here.

But it is through the indeterminacy of its apparent object that sensuous certainty finds itself in its first dilemma: now and here pick out every situation, and so it must either admit external terms as affecting *this* object and excluding others, and thereby admit mediation, or it must find some other way to single out[13] or secure the specificity of its object. In other words, either its object is truly indeterminate, and so a 'now' (or a 'here') that is *all* nows and heres (this is the initial form of universality)[14] but differentiated and mediated through the act of certainty (because this now is *not-then* or *not-there*), or it can uncover another immediate term that can salvage what it means by this now or here.

It is through its being mine that I am certain of the objective field, and so the temporal and spatial order is given up and the order of conscious awareness itself adopted. It should be clear that this option simply reinscribes the problem of mediation: there are as many distinct I-situations as there are now-situations, thus either this I must be mediated by a unified or universal I, singled out from and related to a principle of subjectivity, or it must be apprehended through another immediately singular term.

But it is equally true that the attempt to assert the primacy of the I is already mediated by the failure of the object to win immediacy. The move back to the knowing or certainty itself results from sensuous certainty being repelled[15] from the object. What we can see, as observers committed to pursuing the attempt to secure immediacy in knowing, is that the object alone cannot provide it and that it must include the being receptive of the knower; but that is, again, precisely to convict sensuous certainty of a contradiction.

In attempting to preserve its integrity in the face of an apparent dependence on otherness, and thus on mediation, sensuous certainty has traced the path whose inevitability was plain the moment it introduced distinctions between what it knew and the act of knowing. But it has been shown a subtler truth about conscious life, one which it will explore explicitly in its final attempt to defend the immediacy of its knowing: that in seeking an immediate, or undifferentiated, integrity, it really has been aiming at a kind of universality, the indifferent[16] unity of every apparently distinct term. What it took to be, the immediately specific or singular object or subject of certainty, has instead shown itself not to be. In its place is the immediate simple togetherness of all terms, the only possible object of an immediate knowing. This sensuous certainty identifies as its own act the "relation that remains self-identical."[17]

In asserting the primacy of its relational integrity, of the act from which it mistakenly sought to isolate objective and subjective terms, sensuous certainty has again unwittingly engaged in mediating its immediacy—it identifies as an immediate or simple unity terms which it has experienced as distinct. As we come to see, however, the unity it achieves by actively assimilating all the terms it has exposed within its experience is only to the extent it is equally actively differentiated from the unity of the activity of sensuous certainty as such.

To identify its relational whole, sensuous certainty discards the comparative object and subject terms (this, now, and I) and gives itself over to the singular experience that it is. There is now no longer the desire to distinguish one object from another, or one subject from another, but the simple devotion to the moment of certainty.

It is here that Hegel insists that we be able to point out the truth on which sensuous certainty depends, a move which, it might be maintained, contaminates sensuous certainty, contravening our impartial observation and subjecting it to an external (and hence mediating) demand. To what extent is the call for pointing a violation of the phenomenological process?

It is obvious from the preface and introduction that our observation, as the universal individual prepared to risk our natural assumptions and our self-certain grasp of the world, is an interested one. That is, we are concerned to discover the kind of knowing which results in truth, and our observation of sensuous certainty is always mediated by our interest. At the same time, our interest can only be safeguarded if we allow conscious life to make its own claims and refrain from intervening. Our interest can mediate our observation, but not sensuous certainty's work. The preliminary conception of phenomenology is just that attitude of letting-be the shapes of conscious life and the confidence that in the course of their own specific attachments either some consistent and satisfactory way of relating to otherness will emerge, or that in its place some determinate improvement to the specific commitments of an inadequate form will show itself.[18]

At the same time, the phenomenological approach that we bring to bear on sensuous certainty requires that we become more involved than would mere spectators. Our task is to recover the interestedness that belongs to the life of each form of consciousness, the interestedness of existence which each form has passed beyond to the extent that it has formed itself as a principle organizing its relations with others.[19]

Sensuous certainty is from the beginning a kind of knowing, a way of being open to the world. If its principle contradicts its actions, if sensuous certainty is in fact incapable of securing an object and of moving from potential to enacted truth, then we need to know this, and we need to know why. What the demand for pointing expresses is our concern for its realization, our concern to let it be what it claims for itself by observing it enacting the standards it sets for itself, which include knowing that something is. *It* has made the claim of certainty, and as we have already seen, it cannot successfully preserve or express its certainty with words. It is in this respect that the claim itself has been abandoned as inherently self-contradictory, but the possibility of such an experience has not yet been abandoned.[20] In trying to preserve or express the experience sensuous certainty claims it has, we are driven to the simplest gesture consistent with the goal of singling something out.

The call to point out the content is an attempt to try to experience what sensuous certainty experiences, that is, to have determinate content, certain and true content, immediately, without the demand for written results. We now are no longer concerned with the self-contradictory fate of those who would assert a claim that would be violated by language. We instead are acting on behalf of the experiencing individual and trying to determine whether or not, under the restricted conditions of isolating for ourselves immediate content, such content is even possible—whether there is any content, that is, to be certain *of*.

What happens, however, is that pointing out the content repeats the collapse we have seen in each of the two previous attempts to be sense-certain: namely, that any one act of experiencing must occur in relation to the kind of experiencing, that any act of singling out points to both the context of possible acts (in this case, space and time), implied by the very act of singling out, and to the content determined within the context.

When the now it affirms is pointed out, it is of course a later, an other, now.[21] This second now is then not the now that was meant, but in its sameness to and difference from that first now, it again shows that it really picks out a kind of possible experiencing or a unity of possibly experienced acts, which it must have in order to specify some determinate content.[22]

To secure its experience, sensuous certainty must distinguish it from the stream of awareness which it claims it truly is. Once again, it has to distinguish between this apparently determinate act and the unity of acts that give it being. The act, in other words, only has its determinacy in being both not just this act but the unity it points to and not just the unity of awareness, that is, not just sensuous certainty in principle but just this act of it.

While sensuous certainty recoils from this discovery, we can see that to affirm the experience of universality, which here means the unity of the contextual possibility of all the acts of its kind, is equally to affirm just this context of the plurality of possibly distinct acts. In our pointing, we have implicitly recognized the unity of similar acts, out of which we have determined this one. What sensuous certainty does is to resist recognizing the unity that is the *sine qua non* of generating determinate experiences.[23] Thus sensuous certainty is thrown back against the truth that Hegel announced early in his analysis: "[a]n actual sense-certainty is not merely this pure immediacy, but an *instance* of it."[24] In characterizing as external the context of possible experiencing its meaning depends on, sensuous certainty is engaged in continually contradicting itself.

In the experience we have endeavoured to make our own, we have learned two things about conscious life: first, that any determinate object must be an expression of the unity of the context of possible content, the context that equally preserves its expression, or gives it permanence, its being;[25] second, that conscious life as a cognitive activity must in its acting recognize the mediating context of preservation and enabling, through which it will attain the mediated immediacy of its object.

But our most pressing concern in the self-determining self-comprehension of experiencing is to see how what we have discovered turns up in and for experiencing itself. I turn now to perception, to see how as ordinary consciousness perception takes up sensible aspects and so preserves what is lost to sensuous certainty.

Perception

With perceptual consciousness, we are introduced to the first form of consciousness that presents itself as the necessary result of a development in conscious life itself. To this extent, perceptual consciousness shows itself to be much more adept at managing to get from one exchange to the next than did sensuous certainty. Perception has found what appears to be a way of taking things as they are, taking them as true, while juggling the sensible details of its predecessor and the universal context on the basis of which those details mean something—the manifold unity of the thing.

Indeed, what distinguishes perception as a form of conscious life is its ability to notice things, take discreet aspects as meaningful, as indicators or signs of its proper object, some manifold unity of those aspects, or some thing. Perceptual consciousness knows that the details which are part and parcel of its awareness of its world stand for some thing, or better, that they belong to some thing. They are not just details, they are openings onto things.[26] At the same time, because (like most of us in our nonreflective encounters with others) perception presupposes the active process of determining the relationship of aspect to thing, thus equally presupposes the determinations 'aspect' and 'thing,' it has a precarious grasp of its situation. The unity it takes to be the truth of any aspect is the unity it makes in identifying any aspect perceptually. It is precisely because its object is in fact this process of distinguishing and then relating aspects to a whole, yet is taken to be either the perceived aspect or the intended whole, that perception runs into trouble.[27] Perception depends on not having to account for what is in fact a much more sophisticated set of cognitive operations than singling out might suggest. Perception works to the extent that its familiar prejudices, whose workings exceed the level of cognitive sophistication it can recognize, are not called forth and continue doing their work surreptitiously.[28]

In this sense, what Hegel calls perception is the kind of conscious life in which we all engage in those moments of relaxed attentiveness, in the simple exchanges whose familiarity guarantees (or at least anticipates) success. While it is easy to see how this can be spelled out in straightforward, perceptual ways—the redness tells us that this is an apple, not a pear, the blue coat picks out this person as our friend, and the sweetness tells us that this is sugar, not salt we want for our coffee—it seems clear that slightly more complex indicators are consistent with the kind of noticing that is going on here. So, perceiving consciousness is equally the sight of the basket I take to contain apples, the gait I notice as that of my friend, and the shape of the container that I take to suggest that sugar is inside it. What is common to all of these is the kind of relating-to-a-unity, which takes some perceived aspect or detail as its cue to identify some thing.[29]

The dialectic of perception, whose stages are not my primary focus here, consists of showing that the aspects given to ordinary awareness presuppose and do not account for the determinations they are used to identify, and that from the side of ordinary awareness these determinations lead into contradiction when forced to become explicit. I will address two points: first, that perception is (in the sense I will develop here) inductive in-itself; and second, that the tacit conceptual work underwriting the relative consistency of perception, when forced into its awareness, brings about the death of its object and its way of experiencing. This crisis will lead consciousness to recognize that details alone cannot account for the unity to which they belong, and that the order of explanation must be inverted.

When we look at its conceptual commitments, we can see that perception demonstrates that it has incorporated the crisis of sensuous certainty in its attitude to the target of its awareness, which Hegel calls the property, and the more sophisticated object that target links up with, the thing. Picking up where pointing out left off, perceptual consciousness takes the sensuous aspect by means of which it singles things out to be an expression of a universal or manifold unity, or not just this. The sensuous aspect points to the unity in which it has its being, the unity which preserves it and at the same time determines it as a not just this, or negates it. In noticing this aspect, it posits[30] the existence of an immediate unity of aspects.

Notice that in taking up the unity of the thing as its proper object, perception is performing the first act of determinate negation, and it is the first instance of the logic upon which the development of the science of experiencing depends.[31] The thing is identified as not just this aspect or detail, but the unity given as a detail, a claim which we have seen experiencing demand as a condition of its having determinate content. Sensuous certainty tried to hold fast to just this, and in recognizing the sensible detail as not just this, perception shows itself to be the result of a positive response to experiencing. This it shows to us, and not to itself; to itself, it is just noticing things. We, however, having attempted to experience the immediacy of sensible content, are in a position to recognize the most naive representation of a self-differentiating unity as what experience demands of consciousness in order to occur at all.[32] What this means is that we can recognize that perception emerges inductively. Let me describe what I mean here by induction, in a preliminary way, and what I take to be its relationship to what Hegel calls determinate negation, before returning to the specifics of perception.

Many philosophers and students of philosophy are most familiar with induction in the context of the notorious "problem of induction"—the problem, that is, of making true and necessary claims about a domain defined in terms of its contingency and fragmentation. Induction is supposed to be problematic because it is generative, because it extends what we can claim to know from an instance to a kind or type, without ever really justifying, we are told, that kind of epistemic or metaphysical leap.

But as Max Black, among others, has argued, the purportedly problematic nature of induction, and this instance-type move as well, belong to a very specific philosophic project, one concerned with upholding the deductive paradigms of rationality and necessity. From the work of Descartes onward, the task of epistemology has been to isolate and investigate those aspects of a transcendental subjectivity that ensure that certain formal criteria are met in our judgments—criteria derived from a conception of reason as self-identical. The problem of induction really is as much a problem of deduction—the consequences of a dualistic conception of knowing that guarantees that what is true can only ever be derived from the nature of a self-identical subjectivity, not said of things themselves or of experience in its terms.

But induction has a richer history than is allowed by conventional epistemology. It hasn't always signified the attempt to lend experience a pale version of the rigorous necessity governing thought itself. In Aristotle, for example, there is an account of induction that speaks more directly to the conception that I am arguing animates Hegel's phenomenology. Let me examine Aristotle's account briefly.[33]

In *Posterior Analytics*, Aristotle describes induction in the context of the problem of identifying the source or origin of the discovery of the primary premises by means of which scientific knowledge is both attained and demonstrated. There are two important issues for Aristotle in detailing the process by means of which we acquire the premises: first, that we, like animals, possess some instinctive discriminatory drive and a corresponding capacity for making sense of the world; and second, that the manner of sense-making we call science or knowledge depends on a series of prior and less accurate or less sophisticated approaches to the task of sense-making. That is, our scientific knowledge develops through an attentiveness to the world and to our success in comprehending it.

Aristotle argues that induction is the name, not for some abstractly rational process of conceptual assimilation, but for the series of unifying responses to the world that lead us to science. Though this process begins for us with sensory experience, the "power of systematizing"[34] sensory awareness arises first as memory, then as experience, and then as skill and science. Each is more appropriate to the subtlety of the scientifically comprehended unity of the experienced world, yet each in its own way serves to make possible a kind of coherent involvement in that world, a determinate range of experiencing made possible by a distinctive approach to the issue of systematicity in experience. Induction, for Aristotle, names the process of learning from experience how it demands of us that we unify and comprehend it.[35]

As I have already suggested, the more traditional (empiricist) account of induction typically begs the question as to what form the unity and multiplicity have to take.[36] Empirical observation is said to pick out a number of similar or identical things or events, then infer from them some uniform rule governing their behaviour or identity. The rules which emerge, however, are not rules of the events or things themselves but presupposed rules of so-called rational observation—criteria establishing what counts as the uniformity and repeatability of certain phenomena.[37]

But, as we will see,[38] it isn't simply the predetermined form that unity has to take that distorts inductive inference in its traditional form. Positing one form of mediating unity in experience is, as we have seen in the experience of sensuous certainty, the *sine qua non* of conscious life. The key to induction becoming for-itself as I will define it is its responsiveness to experience under any inadequate principle or rule, when that rule disintegrates in the face of what happens in conscious life. Induction in Hegel's *Phenomenology of Spirit* bears a closer resemblance to what Feyerabend might call counter-induction—the need, prompted by experience itself, to renegotiate our categories.

It is from this standpoint that the dualism posited by and implicit in the traditional form of induction becomes as problematic as its circularity. If experience is defined as comprised of intrinsically discreet units, any unity will necessarily be presupposed (and thus imposed), and from the perspective of experience itself, imposed arbitrarily. Because it is imposed without regard for the object itself, its imposition can only be immediate or unconditioned by the mediating presence of the multiplicity itself. There always will be a "remainder" (or, better, a "reminder") left unaccounted for, because within intrinsically fragmented multiplicities, unity can only tell part of the story. The antithesis between an immediate multiplicity and a knowing unity marks this form of consciousness as inductive in-itself—that is, induction that has not yet learned the unity that reconciles it with, by accounting for, its experienced multiplicity.[39] This accounts for the close relationship between traditional accounts of induction and debates over probability theory, in which contingently related events are rated according to their approximation to a rule.

The conservative nature of epistemological debates on this issue (which have hardly advanced at all) is the result of this dualism, which allows proponents of traditional induction to replicate the dualism within the object, pointing to a rational core over and against a contingent and changing surface, or a regularity amidst discrepancy, and so on. The fact that the project of traditional epistemology is self-critical is diffused in the irregularities built into this unruly beast it has dubbed experience. Even the critics of traditional induction invoke just this dualism to challenge the legitimacy of administering any form of unity. Experience, they say, is made up of indeterminately discreet units, or temporally determined successive contents of consciousness, so no prior conformity between units might be discovered. Hume's famous objections to the importing of inherently abstract conceptual unities (like causal necessity) into the inherently fragmentary world of experiencing are perhaps the clearest expression of what has plagued accounts of induction from the outset of traditional (seventeenth- and eighteenth-century) epistemology: that it has already defined the possible forms of conceptual unity and the necessarily fragmentary nature of experience as opposed.[40]

To be sure, Hume gives no sign of being disturbed by the fact that he was invoking the very opposition presupposed by the abstract-rationalist conception of induction to deny the legitimacy of the practice—to ground a skeptical epistemology and philosophy of mind, in other words. Within contemporary epistemological debates, which typically deal with

Hume's objections, it is of course not the predetermined opposition but its positive reconciliation as question-begging that has come under fire. The so-called problem of induction is the problem of justifying what has to be presupposed for inductive inference to occur. If induction is said to be the gathering of a number of identical units to make some claim about a rule governing their identity, surely that identity has already been at work in making the selection of identical units possible. The move that appears to confirm both the specific induction and the method of inductive inference in general instead confirms the strength of the deductive hypothesis already in place. What appears to be induction is rather a kind of confirmation of a deductive paradigm. This is certainly the case in discussions of so-called scientific method in contemporary epistemology, where the paradigm of calculative or mathematical unities is confirmed, rather than experience observed.[41]

The concept of induction that I am arguing animates Hegel's account of the self-comprehension of experience emerges from two convergent themes in the text's argument: the necessity that we approach truth claims about the nature of experiencing in terms of the experiencing these claims in turn make possible, and the necessity that experiencing develop itself to scientific self-comprehension.[42]

The emphasis on experiencing as the self-determining source of its science is most clearly evident in the introduction, especially in the description of experience as that which develops according to determinate negation. That is, experiencing poses its own demands and acts as its own "principle of verification."[43] Indeed, for Hegel, *this is experiencing*: positing a way of relating to otherness, and a form of otherness itself, and then trying to make sense of the world in light of these posited claims.[44] If a given reflection on experience shows itself to be incapable of organizing what happens as conscious life, that incapacity shows up not only as refuted by experience, but as my having failed to account for some specific aspect of experiencing. According to the description of determinate negation, this concrete expression of failure "is what experience has made of [the prior reflection]," a kind of counter proposal for renewing reflection that comes from experiencing itself.[45]

To the extent that consciousness is prepared to pursue its attempts to know what happens in experiencing, it has been given the determinate expression of what its prior conception lacked. But within any installed principle or rule of experiencing, this expression shows up as the disparity between the object sanctioned by the prior positing of the rule and another unsanctioned object whose appearances destroy the integrity of the rule. Induction by determinate negation means accounting for this new, unsanctioned object by unifying experience inductively, according to the rule that reconciles or accommodates the experienced difference.

The traditional problem of a unit that begs the question of inductive inference is not an issue here (at least not in the traditional way) because the unsanctioned unit and the unity in which it can be reconciled are other than the installed one. From the perspective of the scientist organizing our experience, this is viewed deductively, that is, in terms of the crisis implicit in the relationship between the scientific concept of experience and the particular rule governing the experience in question. But just as it is crucial to the scientist that the concept be the result of a self-development, so too it is crucial that the experience in question *show itself* to be the experience of the difference generated by its own rule for experiencing when it is realized as experiencing. In other words, *what the scientist calls determinate negation is achieved by experiencing consciousness as induction.* Induction is the means by which the experience of one installed rule is overcome, or better, transformed, as a response to the experience that calls for another; it is not the confirmation of what has already been established. It is precisely the failure of the principle to secure experience in its own terms that makes induction both possible and necessary.[46]

Just as it does not beg the question of the units to be unified, induction in the science of experiencing does not predetermine the kind of unity it aspires to, nor is its experienced otherness posited as fragmented in some predetermined opposition to reflective unity.[47] One form of conscious life posits its ultimacy, and it is experience, as the performance of the shape of conscious life, that reveals the need for and the path to transformation. Induction names the originary role played by experiencing in all of its manifestations, its role in working out its own unifying principle and as the context in which the success of any reflection on that experiencing is to be measured.[48] Induction, and not the deduction of a given concept, is the logic that ensures that the development here is the self-mediation of experiencing consciousness.

To pursue experiencing in its truth, then, consciousness must learn to read in its experiencing the appearance of an unsanctioned difference and be prepared not only to see in this difference some further signs of progress, but also (the two are inseparable) to experience its own limits as already transgressed.[49] To actualize its progress, consciousness must transform these signs (typically, the difference between what it thought it knew and what its experience has shown to be its proper object), to unify them, as a new kind of knowing. Induction by determinate negation is transformative in pursuing the fragmentation that occurs as a result of an inappropriate approach to its experience. In learning to read its own experiencing, in order to unify as a reflective principle what really happens in experiencing, consciousness must be inductive, which is to say it must let its experience direct it and be prepared to forego familiarity and those other forms of conceptual stasis and expose itself, or make itself vulnerable, to the threatening context of instability and contingency.

It is equally true, however, that the bulk of Hegel's transitions (for this is where we see the inductive moment of the logic of experiencing most clearly, in the movement toward a new reflection) occur accompanied by the reassuring presence of the scientist himself. To what extent has Hegel's argument, and thus the very claim about experiencing providing its own argument, already been compromised in its presentation as completed? Where might we find the inductive risk in the controlled (and often intrusive) tone of the scientist, which testifies however implicitly to the deductive element in what we are reminded repeatedly is already a scientific argument?

This is clearly a very serious question and one to which a number of commentators have devoted many pages of commentary. Without entering into any one of these debates specifically, let me redescribe in this context what I consider the distinctively inductive element.[50]

There are two processes of development that need to be distinguished here. One is what Hegel frequently refers to as a "past" which is already completed.[51] The other is the one we as readers, or better as thinkers,[52] are undertaking, a development Hegel will call, referring in part to the Socratic account of learning by *anamnesis*, the recollection or *Erinnerung* of the first development.[53]

There are two kinds of transitions that figure into the narrative of experiencing: the transition made by the experiencing consciousness, which at some time held one of these views as its own, and the transition we are experiencing as necessary in our recollection. About the first of these, it seems we can say very little, other than what must have happened insofar as any one form of consciousness always presupposes development. Hegel will, from time to time, describe these transitions as improbable, as he does, for example, in the case of sensuous certainty.[54]

In our transitions, however, we are demanding of ourselves that we let only the experienced expression of the determinate breakdown of any one shape of consciousness be our guide, and the only necessity that governs our development is the necessity of an inductive unification of that experienced breakdown. The experience of a form of conscious life is not to be taken as expressive of a given concept of experience, affirming what we have already been told, but as making possible a specific development, making that advance necessary for experiencing to show its truth completely.

In this sense, then, we are engaged in the transcendental induction of the concept of experience, where experiencing itself expresses to us the unifying principle with which it is to be comprehended. That this process has been organized scientifically in no way detracts from the originary role experiencing itself plays. To pursue the course of the argument, we need to experience each form of conscious life, to address it in in terms of the experience it allows and to find in that experience alone our basis for developing further.

At the same time, as I have already remarked, this process is deductive from the standpoint of the scientist. In focusing on what I call the transcendental induction of the concept of experience, I am not claiming to exclude the role of deduction here.[55] Rather than threaten the inductive element, however, the role of deduction in Hegel's science makes clear its dependence on induction, that is, on the experience of consciousness itself as the source of its scientific concept. The scientific deduction is the demonstration of its legitimacy in claiming to comprehend the self-comprehension of experience, but its presentation as a series of inductions equally confirms the legitimacy of each of the inductive moves and the necessity of inductive inference in general.[56] Experiencing consciousness does not have the concept given to it, but must wrest it free from its own experiencing. What experiencing demands in order to be comprehended is not simply posited, but experienced. The reciprocal entailment of induction and deduction, of a concept that shows itself to have emerged as the self-development of the phenomenon of experiencing, is the distinctively dialectical element of Hegel's concept of experience.[57] It is because the concept of experience is its own self-comprehension that its inductive emergence belongs to it essentially, which is just what the phenomenological scientist has recognized in presenting its self-development inductively.

The transcendental induction in which we are engaged allows us to make some additional observations about each of the forms of conscious life that we come across in our development, precisely because we have experienced their origins, undergone what lends them the necessity they claim as their own. In different contexts, this amounts to different kinds of observations; one of the most compelling, however, and one that holds true for all but one (the ultimate one) of the forms, is the extent to which each has "forgotten" the experience on which it depends for its necessity. As each claims to be the truth of experiencing, their indebtedness to what has gone before them ought to, but doesn't, figure in that truth. In one way or another, each posits some immediate ground for its truth, some noninductive principle. At almost every point in the argument, the difference between "we" (the reader committed to bringing each principle to life and to seeing the experience through) and "it" (the experience of each principle itself) is precisely our awareness that experience has led it to embrace the necessity of its principle, that it is the result of induction. While each form of experiencing prior to absolute knowing posits an immediate antithesis between its principle and the multiplicity it organizes, and thereby shows itself to be inductive only in-itself, we can see how its experience of a prior multiplicity mediates that immediacy. What distinguishes us, then, is our retrospective recognition of the inductive origins of each shape of conscious life.[58] My argument throughout this work will be focused on the gradual awakening of consciousness to this indebtedness to its experiencing, this history, which only phenomenology will adequately recognize.

There are two reasons for emphasizing perceptual consciousness' indebtedness to experiencing. The first of these concerns the transcendental induction which I am arguing that the *Phenomenology of Spirit* enacts: namely, the self-mediating self-comprehension of experiencing consciousness. It is because experiencing consciousness shows itself to depend on self-mediation to occur at all that the goal of self-comprehension, or the self-unification of the terms uncovered in self-mediation, becomes a scientific objective. It is, in other words, only because experience shows itself to be more than what immediately appears that the issue of the "more" becomes both the possible and, as we shall see, the necessary object of the science of experiencing.

The second issue concerns perceiving consciousness specifically. Perception is that form of consciousness which first tacitly acknowledges the role of mediation and experiences things as unified or universal. What we can say now is that this is a response to the experience which asserted itself in our attempt to make sensuous certainty live up to its pronounced truth. Experiencing itself has already mediated what experiencing consciousness claimed simply "is" or "happens," thus we can see now that it only happens if its most primitive demands have already been incorporated into the organizing principle of experiencing consciousness. Perceiving consciousness is inductive to the extent that we can see in it the simplest unification (or objectification, in this case) of what we experienced as the difference between determinate content and a preserving and enabling unity of determinateness.[59]

Notice I am not claiming that it knows itself to be inductive or has practiced some kind of experiment with sensuous certainty. Rather, what we saw in experiencing sensuous certainty was that in its simplest terms experiencing demanded a manifold unity of possible experiences in order to have determinate content in any act of conscious life. That demand is reflected as having been met by perception, thus in perception we find the expression of what is for us the first lesson of experiencing; we see, in other words, where the necessity of perceiving things lies.

This inductive pre-history is precisely what Hegel refers to in the introduction, as the necessity "that presents itself to consciousness without its understanding how this happens, which proceeds for us, as it were, behind the back of consciousness."[60] "Behind its back" is just what our transcendental induction enables us to say about the necessity animating perception: it takes itself to be necessary, but we can see that in-itself, perception is necessary only for experiencing to develop itself from itself.

Indeed, the disparity between the necessity it reflects in its behavior and the necessity it attaches to things is the basis for the experienced collapse of perception. The unity it must have is posited as the immediate unity of sensible or perceptible details. But perceptible details point to any number of unities, or at least cannot be said to point to any one to the exclusion of others, making perception haphazard at best.[61] Let me turn to the experience of perceiving consciousness and to its posited unity to develop the crisis in perception.

There are two consequences that follow from this positing. The first is that it must posit many other properties, each of which is like the first—mediated by the unity that preserves and makes them all accessible. This is what consciousness learned from sensuous certainty: that the unity that preserves and enables its experience is the unity of all the related experiences it preserves and makes possible, thus to recognize it is to posit an indeterminate number of aspects.

Seen from the perspective of their common ground, the many properties emerge as immediately one with it. Yet they are its determinate and differentiated expressions, determined and differentiated as other than the unity in which they are preserved. The many properties are themselves locked into a kind of logical isolation, having each come forth from the simple unity as nothing more determinate than details co-posited with the manifold.

The instances are indifferent to one another because the common ground in which they are preserved and which makes them available to perception is indifferent to their determinate diversity. In this respect, perception has followed sensuous certainty, for which the now that is noon and the now that is midnight are themselves related only as nows; they carry no reference to the specificity of each other in themselves. They find their being simply in the belonging to a universal that is equally unaffected by the specifics of its moments. The moments are distinct only as constitutive of a manifold or universal togetherness. Because they are 'generic' expressions, their only determinateness lies in their pointing necessarily to a higher unity and in their being *not* each other.

At this conceptual level, we can see that the mutual indifference of the properties poses a problem for perceiving consciousness. The plurality of self-related properties must have some common element if they are to relate as properties to the one unity which preserves them—if they are, that is, to be *proper* to it and it alone. It isn't sufficient to say that there are 'these other' determinate expressions of this thing; the phrase 'these other expressions' picks out the whole field of perceptible qualities itself, or all white things, for example, as much as it picks out any one white thing.[62]

So perception has to mean more than this; it means those other properties to be the specific determinacies *proper to* the manifold of things: shape, texture, and so on. But once again, these determinations belong to many things, while perception means this determinate thing, this white, round thing, for example, and not that one, which is round, white, and sour, for example. Things of perception are supposed to be distinguished, singled out, by their properties, which means that the thing has to be further determined as having a principle of exclusion, as being itself this one and not another.

Thus, as a second consequence of the initial positing of the object, the many determinacies now have to be turned against one another. To be properties, the many determinacies must somehow belong together, which means they must both distinguish themselves from one another and relate themselves to each other as not that other *thing*.[63] The properties cannot be themselves in the simple unity of the manifold, the passive universality of sensuous certainty. The distinct terms of the Thing's oneness must be actively differentiating themselves from each other and from the other Things whose properties they are not.

On the basis of the singling out of properties, then, no principle of exclusion can ever be articulated without making some reference to at least the experiential context of the conscious individual. Exclusion determines this white and round thing over and against others, so it implicitly subverts the intended immediacy of the one. Perception, then, constructs these two barriers to its own success: the principle of exclusion on which its determinate thing depends cannot be a property of the thing, thus the thing cannot really be a one, let alone be perceived.

Perceiving consciousness, in other words, has gone from the apparent immediacy of a property that is in and through its determinate universality, the Thing, to a property whose relationship to its Thing is the result of an intricate conceptual mediation, invoking both the entire field of perceptible qualities *and* the ultimately *im*perceptible field of relations between things. Needless to say, this is a maze through which the specific property, in the simple act of perceptual reference, is unlikely to lead us, and which perception itself is unwilling to enter.

Perception, like ordinary consciousness in general, recognizes the relatively sophisticated determination of its object as opposed to the act through which it apprehends it. It recognizes that, given the diversity of aspects given to its attention and the criterion of oneness it hopes to gather from them, it is liable to make mistakes, or be deceived. What it doesn't see, but we have already seen, is that regardless of its success rate, its project is at best contingent, and at worst self-defeating; the many cannot of themselves be *perceived* as the kind of one they have to be.

In the experience of perceiving that we observe, it is precisely the frustration of trying to hold fast to the one that brings out the specific commitments (to the many elements of its experiential context and to this context as the unity that can accommodate something like a principle of exclusion) on which it is founded and with which it will be able to develop into the more comprehensive cognitive stance called understanding.

Hegel distinguishes three stages in the experience of perception, beginning with the initial recognition of the untenability of the perceptual act itself. Sensuous aspects do not secure the oneness of the thing; rather, the sensuous aspects dissolve the oneness, which can only be maintained as what consciousness means by singling out a property. The act of recognizing that meaning is a relation mediated by a universal has now collapsed back into sensuous certainty because the unity through which this sensuous aspect is preserved is not itself determinate. It has many properties, and in failing to determine which ones it has and which it doesn't by relying on details, perception is forced to abandon its intrinsic multiplicity and is thrown back to proclaiming that this one property is enough. If the only determinate feature of the one thing is this one property, the one is really just this property *as* the thing. The thing then names the sensuous being with which sensuous certainty mistakenly sought communion.

The subsequent stages in its experience are important to our advancement beyond perception, because perceiving consciousness is driven to introduce two crucial claims: the first, which results from consciousness taking on itself either the aspect of oneness or the aspect of multiplicity, is that the thing has two ways of being itself; the second is that these two ways of being together make up the unity which consciousness has to take for its object, a unity that extends beyond its perceptible awareness.[64]

The claim that the thing is really duplicitous arises from the attempt to get past the initial collapse back into sensuous certainty. From the outset, the possibility of deception has been explicit for the perceiving individual. What is implicit in deception is the active involvement through which the perceiver connects the property to the intended thing. Its initial breakdown makes this involvement explicit and deception a function of the necessary role consciousness plays. Failure, then, is assigned to its having initiated its own deception in its involvement in recognizing the thing.

The goal now is to undo the damage caused by the intervention of consciousness. The oneness of the thing is maintained in spite of the emergence of distinct properties, and those properties are explained on the basis of the individual's perceptual manifold: I encounter many because my sensuous awareness is conditioned by many organs of apprehension. The one, now reduced to an empty determination, vanishes. It must be these properties, because to be a thing is to be as the unity of the sensuous aspects. It is one because it is its properties; but so determined, it is the medium of this property and that one, and so on.

The unity having again dissolved, consciousness now takes responsibility for it by turning one property against another, by acting, in other words, as the moment of negation. It sets properties apart insofar as each is not the other, thereby overcoming the threat of dissolution. The thing is now a housing fashioned by the perceiving individual and not the object of perception at all.[65]

In the back and forth of oneness and its dissolution, between the perceiver and what it takes to be its object, the thing has been explicitly assigned the two (still implicitly contradictory) ways of being that we anticipated above: it is the indeterminate medium in which the many properties find their independence and the one which is supposed to be both determinate and determining. This can come as no surprise to us, because from the beginning, any one thing has depended on each of these two contradictory dimensions of thinghood. Given its failure to trade off responsibility for the crisis with the object, and especially given its object-orientation, consciousness assigns these two ways of being to the thing.

Consciousness already has given the basis for dividing the being of the thing. On the one hand, the thing is for consciousness, or for another, a diversity; but on the other hand, the thing is itself a one. This initial take on the thing's twofold being slips right back into chaos: the thing must still somehow unify its two aspects, but it is consciousness that makes the distinction and restores the unity, not the thing.

To give the divided things objective being, consciousness has to claim that the unity or oneness remains the true being of the thing, a oneness that is disturbed by another thing. It is in the context of other things, then, that problems of identity emerge, but by itself, the thing remains one.

Once the context of things has become an explicit component of the thing's being, perception is effectively finished. From the beginning, it has attempted to cling to the independence of the thing, insisting on its autonomy again and again in the face of the ties between its distinguishing properties and the field of perceptibility. Now, perception has admitted that the thing is constituted by its determinateness, by its oneness, but at the same time that the determinate features of its constitution reach beyond it into a comprehensive manifold of determinate properties. To have a thing at all will be to attempt to maintain the distinction between its singularity and the perceptible field, even if one is called (initially) unessential. To do that, however, will require a new level of awareness that goes beyond insisting on the immediacy of the singular object, one that can get beyond the affirmation of this thing underlying this property and address the comprehensive context in which things appear—the mediating and constitutive manifold itself. It will require something more than taking things to be true; it will require a kind of making, the construction of the appropriate determining context which allows things to appear as such. It will require, in other words, that consciousness have as its object what perception has been doing, not what it has perceived as true.

Conclusion

In the first part of this chapter, I argued that sensuous certainty proves incapable of delivering its promise of an immediately self-verifying experience. But that failure of immediacy takes the form of an indication of what kind of mediation experiencing requires, and it is as having learned that lesson from experience, or as resulting from an implicitly inductive relationship to experience, that we must investigate the experience of perception.

In following the dialectic of perception, we have seen the goal of a consistent cognitive attitude to otherness determined further. For perception, the tension between its desire to make sense of its object and the need for a more comprehensive and aggressive approach to otherness is reflected in its frustration, when pressed, to identify what it means without going beyond and thereby subverting the independence of its intended object. Its desire, expressed in its insistence on the thing that its property indicates, animates its experience and is frustrated by the limits of its cognitive sophistication. What it requires to bring about its satisfaction is a different kind of openness to its world.

Like sensuous certainty, then, the possibility that perception could continue as a way of living in the world depends on its suppression of the kind of reflection opened up by its repeated frustration. Its very survival, in other words, depends on not thinking about itself. But what its cycle of failed experiences has led it to is precisely its death: the need to reach beyond what is merely taken as truth to actively comprehend perceptible details in thought.

In the next chapter, I will pursue the development of conscious life as thinking, as a way of making more of its perceptual experience. What this will initiate, then, is the recognition that the experience of objects depends on a prior commitment to a conceptual unity,[66] which must then be reconstructed in order to grasp the determinate object as such; it is a recognition that will in the course of making it good drive conscious life into the crisis of skeptical despair.

CHAPTER TWO

Understanding, Desiring, and Death

Introduction

In the last chapter, I argued that the disparity between what ordinary consciousness does in singling out its object and what it takes to be true in that activity results in a (self-)critical instability. Things are one, and they are many; there is nothing in the perceptible detail with which perception concerns itself to secure the unity and with it perceptual success. In this chapter, I look at two ways of experiencing which, having experienced the tension in ordinary consciousness, make comprehensive claims about unifying the necessary moments of oneness and multiplicity. They are ways, then, of explicitly interpreting the whole of experiencing.

The first of these is what Hegel calls the understanding. Its experience as described phenomenologically is both intricate and unwieldy and at times further complicated by Hegel's use of what were at one time popular scientific notions. I will focus the analysis by emphasizing, from the outset, the two primary lessons its experience will offer: first, that the unity of oneness and multiplicity must be a *self-differentiating* unity, that is, it cannot collapse the difference between the moments in the name of the simple unity that was the undoing of perception; and second, that this self-differentiating unity belongs, not to things, but to the experiencing individual.[1]

The second form of comprehensive unification, which emerges directly from the experience of the understanding, is that form of individual consciousness which *immediately* identifies itself as that self-differentiating unity: desiring self-consciousness. Both the density of Hegel's analysis of desiring self-consciousness and its place in the transition to the shapes of consciousness which take selfhood to be the truth of all that is experienced make this an equally complex passage in the argument, and I will again focus my reading on the lesson it offers: namely, that selfhood cannot be immediately reflected as the truth of its experience, but must instead be the result of experience reflecting itself. Therefore, desiring self-consciousness has to learn how to recognize this reflection of self in an independent, self-determining experience; it must come to recognize its dependence on experience for learning about the truth of its selfhood; in other words, it must learn to be inductive for-itself.

The Experience of the Understanding

I already have suggested that a preoccupation with the presence of terms from the theoretical physics of Hegel's era obscures to some extent the experience of the understanding. Some commentators have picked up on this presence and treated the chapter as if it were an analysis of scientific consciousness.[2] There are good reasons for using the concepts of certain theoretical approaches to the natural world as exemplary here, particularly because the tendency to apply highly abstract theoretical constructs to phenomena that are "purely" natural is part of the bravado of the understanding. But it is not exclusively scientific. Hegel, in his preface, cites a number of different examples that equally reflect its central claim: that the truth of experiencing is to be found in thought.[3]

The metaphysical commitment informing the cognitive stance adopted by the understanding is an immediate dualism of sensible experience and conceptual truth. If we cannot perceive the unities the truth demands because what we actually perceive is this or that explosion of properties,[4] argues the understanding, then the truth of those properties must lie somewhere else, where it is unaffected by the perceived multiplicity. This positing of a mutual exclusivity between what is experienced, perceived, and thought, and the co-posited *comprehension* of what is perceived by what is thought, is the tension which drives the experience of the understanding toward crisis. It is the phenomenon of abstract explanation that we are addressing here.

In understanding things, then, we are attempting to reflect on the unity of the perceived multiplicity, a reflection which takes the form of overriding what is posited as intrinsically many in order to arrive at the unity our experience has identified as the truth, a unity expressed in an abstract concept.

The experience of the understanding is complex in part because of its gradual emergence from the experience of ordinary consciousness.[5] The emergence itself is conditioned by the understanding's characteristic intransigence, its reluctance to recognize that it comes from somewhere or that it is subject to development of any kind. Holding fast to an abstract unity that is dependent on its exclusion of, or more appropriately its opposition to, the perceived multiplicity, the understanding is not prepared to account either for where it has come from or where its conceptual commitments will take it. It has won itself the security perception lacked by shifting the issue from one of apprehension to one of comprehension, and its unity is predicated on the exclusion of the kinds of concerns that mark perception.

Hegel remarks on this in the paragraph introducing the understanding. Specifically, he warns us to be wary of the understanding's tendency to refuse responsibility for the unity called for by comprehension, which is to say the unity of thought and what it is thought of. This is the unity that thought claims to have as the truth *of* the perceptual multiplicity, the unity, that is, of the difference between unity and multiplicity implicit in the project announced as *comprehensive*. Specifically, we are to watch for that unity to be posited by the understanding as an exclusive difference.[6] Because the understanding traffics in concepts that are defined by their indifference to experience, concepts that once established enjoy a familiarity and self-evidence because of their applicability under any circumstances, we are to step into its experiences and push it beyond immediate acceptability. As was the case for our involvement with sensuous certainty, we are not to take the reflections of the understanding at face value, but as a way of experiencing we must bring to life. The understanding claims to have comprehended experience, and our task is to discover just what it really means to experience the world 'understandingly.' We are to push it to its extreme, in other words, a move that will reveal its hidden dependence on experiencing, if only to those of us prepared to survive its self-contradiction.[7]

The understanding, in the experience we are to engage in, will reveal the same disparity between what it does and what it claims it has as its truth that we have seen in the experience of perception and sensuous certainty. In the process, it will reveal just what kind of difference really obtains between unity and multiplicity and how that difference is at the same time a kind of unity, the unity experiencing demands of its self-comprehension.

I will divide the chapter into three parts corresponding to the experiential stages I have just marked: (1) the emergence of thinking as the activity equal to the task of unification; (2) the recognition that concepts must take the form of law and that the perceived multiplicity is the appearance of laws; and (3), the crisis of explanation according to law-governed behavior.

THE EMERGENCE OF THINKING

Hegel argues that ordinary consciousness ends up flipping back and forth between universal or essential units, or things, and the aspects which no longer secure them. It is a slightly more refined commonsense empiricism, which refuses to give up the details of sense, but which admits as its real object imperceptible entities. The back and forth of its behavior is never really described in terms of a pivotal crisis, but rather as a self-defeating and humiliating instability or confusion.

The understanding is at first nothing more than the recognition that the imperceptible objects of ordinary consciousness demand to be met head on and sorted out.[8] In trying to bring the notions of essence, unity, single detail, and so on together, the understanding has implicitly taken on in thought the task of sorting out what is true in the experience of perception.

The significance of the move out of perception is that thought has *identified* the terms that were experienced as repeatedly confronting and undermining each other: the independent unity the thing was supposed to hold and the determinate multiplicity of properties by means of which it won that independence, by distinguishing itself from other things. However, for perception the latter contradicted the posited independence by subjecting it to a comparative or relative self-identity achieved by means of the properties that belonged to it and to no other; for the understanding these terms must somehow belong together to be aspects of the same entity.

There are two consequences for the understanding in positing this unity as the "unconditioned universal." First, it means that whatever the thing is as a unit, it is so as related to others. Its identity is therefore *contextually* determined, and so context is the proper object of the understanding.[9] At the same time, this is not simply a conceptual overview of the identity of the thing, of how it comes to be this thing, but a claim about what the thing *really* is. Both the context, and the thing as a detail of context, are now wholly appropriated by conceptual determinations. The thing is no longer the property of perception, but a detail of the understanding. Unity now belongs both to the context, as expressed in a multiplicity of determinate things, and to the context as the truth in which those determinations lose their seeming independence.

In other words, the very difference the understanding has posited as overcome, the difference between the two sides of perceiving, reappears as the two kinds of unity Hegel sets out in the opening paragraph of the chapter. There is a unity that knows no differences, the unity of the determining context *over and against* its multiple expressions, and the unity *of* those expressions, the more intricate unity as differentiated.

For the understanding, these are two aspects of the conceptual unity it has won, each of which appears in a process of alternation. To be the unity that is the truth of differences, Force, the name the understanding knows this process by, must show itself as a context or field of differences and then be confirmed *qua* unity as the unity underlying that field.[10] This is the erosion of the understanding's responsibility, performed as the emphasis on the unity of unity and the suppression of the difference presupposed by unity as a *result*.

In this process, however, the uncontrolled alterity of perception threatens to reassert itself because each of the two moments necessarily implies the other, and each assertion of its difference from the other challenges the unity posited by the understanding. The understanding saves itself from making the kinds of arbitrary and self-defeating distinctions raised in the experience of its predecessor by unifying its object *again*: Force must include both these moments, of context of differences and context as unity, that is, as a unity *reflected* out of *difference* (the difference between the two domains it works with) as the *inner being* of things.[11]

Again, however, difference threatens to scuttle the whole project. There is no way of accounting for a reflected unity without giving the different constitutive moments a legitimate place, as what it takes to be reflected, thereby admitting difference to be part of the very being of unity.[12] The understanding, which cannot recognize the kind of difference now erupting at each turn, collapses the difference between the context of differences and the context as unity by positing each as the fulfilment of the other in the second order unity of a movement of reciprocal determination.[13] The understanding chooses to emphasize the movement in which the terms or moments immediately reflect each other (and not in which real differences reflect some third relation); that is, the understanding refuses the complexity of a unity in which the unity of the context is implicated in the context as differentiated, and vice versa. Instead, it sticks to its claim that this movement, the imperceptible or supersensible movement of reciprocal determination, is the immanent or inner unity of things.

As a result, the immediate unity of things-in-context and contextual determination as such is replaced by a second order, immediate unity that shows itself to have been wholly abstracted from the experiential component that was a remnant of perception. There is no longer any need to put into play the kind of distinctions that the understanding was driven to in order to protect its unity, for example, distinction between form and content and between invisible conceptual moments and aspects of the experienced field. The reciprocity of any distinguished moments is subordinated to the unity that is reciprocity itself. This is not so much of a concern, perhaps, from the side of the formal distinctions that were made, but it is an issue to the extent that we have now overcome the difference between formal moments and experienced moments by positing a unity that is actual only in thought.[14]

The movement of Force into and out of determinate contexts is our object, but it is now, by virtue of the immediate identification of the two moments so disruptive of the perceived context, a unity *mediated*, or *conditioned*, by the exclusion of its own difference. The context as determinate is instead an *appearance*, which names both a *totality* of perceived differences and its having been unified and identified as other than what is true. The object of the understanding is the objectively mediated inner being of things, and understanding consciousness has once again revealed its dependence on the role of perceptual experiencing: the tension between unity and multiplicity in perception has its truth in a supersensible world whose permanence is the truth of what vanishes in mediation and whose unity is the truth of the totality that appears.[15]

With this move into a world of intelligible reality, a world that is posited as the truth of what is experienced by ordinary consciousness, the understanding has been forced to make explicit both its rejection of the perceptible realm and its inability to discard it completely. The truth *of* appearances continues to reflect a dependence on what perceiving consciousness takes to be true, however much the understanding claims its truth lies elsewhere. The appearance belongs, according to the understanding, to ordinary consciousness, for whom it represents a cognitive limit; but we recognize that appearance equally belongs to that of which it is the appearance, to the inner being which necessarily appears in just this way, thus *we* see that the understanding has again tacitly announced responsibility for the content of ordinary consciousness.[16]

In this gradual emergence from its explicit involvement with the world of ordinary consciousness, to its claim to have left it behind, the understanding progressively sharpens its already antagonistic relationship to the experience of perception. For the understanding, the fragmentary disclosure of perceptible properties is the problem, and it is one that cannot and must not affect the contextual or comprehensive approach adopted in seeking to understand appearances. Things that are defined by the activity of ordinary experiencing, with its limited perspective, cannot be unified even to the extent necessary to assign them a constant identity. Unity instead demands of consciousness that it recognize an imperceptible or supersensible order of reality which is the inner unity of what appears, or of objectivity itself.

The movement away from the thing and its properties then is more importantly a move away from recognizing the significance of experiencing itself, a significance we have already seen and which has enabled us to define perception in terms of induction. In positing an inner being that is already the unity of what might turn up differently in experiencing, and in assigning to appearance the multiplicity which has shown itself to be one moment in the experience of ordinary consciousness, the understanding declares its independence from experiencing.

The prior unity the understanding seeks in sorting out the contradictory objects of perception is, for us, already present in perceptual experience. That is, perceptual experience shows *itself* to be the source of the dichotomous relationship between things and properties, in its positing a universal beyond some perceptible detail. Moreover, we know where that positing originated and why: it was the minimum requirement of experiencing, which demanded a relationship between each detail and the unity that preserved it and made it accessible to consciousness. The unity of the terms of perceptual consciousness lies in its implicitly inductive relationship to experiencing as such.

But in objectifying this unity and by translating the terms of the perceptual experience into purely intelligible ones, the understanding has declared its refusal to take experience into account, except insofar as it is an aspect that unified objectivity gives to us, a *derived* multiplicity, precisely because for it experience means the muddle from which ordinary consciousness hasn't successfully extricated itself.

The understanding is already, as we have seen, dependent on experiencing. In fact, despite its hostility to the experiential flux of perception, the understanding is itself inductive, in two ways. First, the necessity of positing a comprehensive unity is precisely what the experience of perception called for: a way of organizing the disparity between sensible details and the supersensible roles they were assigned in discriminating between units, or things. The move into the understanding is, as I have described above, a sorting out of the determinations which crop up in perception and which seem to have a kind of independence from any specific content. Taking that side of the experience of perception as its guide, the understanding unifies it in the form of the posited unity of all of the moments distinguished in perception. Again, in calling the understanding inductive in this respect I am arguing, with Hegel, that the possibility and necessity of its posited intelligible unity is something that arises only on the basis of the experience of ordinary consciousness, which is forced to make explicit the kinds of unities it really recognizes in juggling sensible details. Notice that its inductive relationship to the experience of ordinary consciousness is precisely what it cannot shake off in its quest for a conceptually secure unity: namely, that of which it is the unity, an experience divided between sensibility and intelligibility. It is responsible for the truth of what happens in experiencing, and no amount of conceptual fortification can eradicate the activity of perceiving.[17] The experience of the understanding is crucial for the inductive development I am recounting, precisely because, in opposing itself to the experience of perception, the experience that made understanding things necessary, it demonstrates what becomes of purely positive conceptions of objective knowledge.

This fortification or development within the experience of understanding as I have been describing is also inductive. The simple unity it posits has by no means solved all the problems of ordinary consciousness. It must answer to the same basic criterion to which each of the forms of conscious life are submitted: ordering and making sense of experience. Here, the simple unity has shown itself to require further determination. The two aspects of force, their unification as the movement of a deeper unity, and finally the distinction between the sensible appearance and its supersensible truth, have all been responses to experience in which some further refinement has been necessitated and accommodated.

To be sure, what I am calling the experience animating the development is not something that "happened" to understanding consciousness at one time or another, but the experience entailed by the kind of posited unity the understanding organizes its experience around. As Hegel suggests early on, our involvement here in provoking and carrying out the development of the object of the understanding is especially important because of its tendency to resist movement and retreat to any abstract unity. The experience in question, then, is the life given to the object by our involvement, the experience of the concept of unity-as-identity. While the understanding itself typically refuses to take the kind of responsibility we have demanded of it here for its thoughts, we are learning the extent to which the understanding remains subject to the demands of experiencing by actualizing that demand ourselves.

THE REALM OF LAW AND THE ROLE OF APPEARANCE

With the subordination of the two moments whose recurring presence has destabilized it, the understanding reaches a kind of plateau and seemingly realizes itself as an internally consistent approach to interpreting experience. What remains to be seen is just how this movement of force is given content and how its relationship to appearance is defined. There are two stages to this further refinement of the understanding, prior to its collapse into crisis. In the first, it acknowledges the mediating role of appearance by concerning itself with appearance as the appearance of laws. The difference between these two terms, however, leads it once again to revise its claim toward an independence from appearance. Its concern then becomes the laws of appearance, and it is through the experience of the fully self-legislating understanding that the problem of tautology arises.

In its focus on the primacy of the movement of reciprocally determining moments, the understanding allows the two moments distinguished either formally or in terms of content, the context as unity and the context as field of determinate differences, to take on the status of appearances. That is, each appears as a moment necessary to the being of force, but the commitment to a universal identity in thought explains that appearance in terms of universality itself.

Remember that the very concept of appearance was used by the understanding to reconcile the multiplicity it repeatedly confronted in its efforts to construe experience in terms of identity. Multiplicity and difference began as roughly comparable terms, with the multiplicity of determinate things in their context a difference the understanding hoped to unify. This multiplicity took many forms, but in the process of developing its object in terms of identity, the understanding recognized any difference whatsoever as an intolerable excess. As a result, 'any difference whatsoever' came to stand for the original multiplicity as that which required unification, and the two terms became synonymous for the understanding.

Appearance was the name given to the two moments inherited from perception and whose legacy plagued attempts to consolidate that inheritance: the context as both unified and differentiated.[18] In naming this ineradicable difference as appearance, the understanding opposed to it its own truth as an inner or intelligible identity not subject to the back and forth of perceptual experience. The metaphysical or ontological move into thought was supposed to liberate it from the differences associated with the opposition of the sensible and the intelligible.

But if this difference is unreal in the realm of the understanding, it remains a difference that belongs to its universal as what appears. No matter how successfully the term appearance already collapses the moments it contains, it still presents itself in relation to, or as different than, universality. Insofar as appearance has already been defined as that which is the other proper to the universal, or that in which the self-identical universal appears as the difference already unified, it is clear that the very notion of universality operative in understanding consciousness is the universal as unity *of* difference. Difference, then, is not some disposable feature of a tainted legacy in ordinary consciousness but something sanctioned by its having to have been overcome by the universal itself. Unity only is as the unity of differences, and even in assigning one-sided primacy to the moment of unity the understanding is driven to recognize the difference universality presupposes as unified. This difference, which Hegel calls "universal difference," is itself bridged by the understanding with the *law* of force.[19]

What the concept of the law does here is to unite in a formal or abstract way the alternating moments the understanding has struggled with *as* moments appropriate to the universal; with law, the understanding unites the two moments by means of the relation of governance. In its abstractness, we can see the loss of the experience of progressively sharpening these moments and the various determinate terms assigned them in that experience. According to the concept of law, all are merely governed differences or appearances. It is only when this abstractness is forced to answer to concrete experiencing that it will show itself to be unstable.

If the law is to serve as "the *stable* image of unstable appearance,"[20] the supersensible world of law is both inertly self-identical and differentiated in accordance with the perceived world. Although it has unified the differences between the two expressions of context, it has not unified the multiplicity of phenomena in any given context and is present in it as its stable reflection.

In this respect, then, the world as it appears remains as an independent and determining force, or as Hegel remarks, it is not yet appearance. Posited as the appearance of the laws, the range of perceived phenomena still requires that it be comprehended as law-governed, thus the understanding is confronted with the task of unifying the perceptible world *as* the appearance of the laws.

For the understanding, then, the differences between things returns as something to be reckoned with, a multiplicity of determinate or concrete differences not yet resolved into the universal difference of an apparent multiplicity. From the experience of this multiplicity, which has been posited as the appearance of the law, there ought to be any number of laws covering details or aspects of the multiplicity. But what the concept of law has not yet done is to account for what kinds of appearances or laws there are, thus the experienced multiplicity suggests "indefinitely *many* laws."[21]

To preserve the notion of law as the unity of universal difference, then, the escalation of potential law-governed situations (the escalation of differences) is shut down by the positing of one universal law. The understanding again rejects the experienced multiplicity, even in the name of the law, and replaces it with the idea of law itself *as* an explanation of the truth of what is experienced.[22]

From the standpoint of affirming the universal or general law, any specific law now takes on the status of a mere appearance of the law. That is, it presents itself as a determinate difference from unity. But any such difference is already described by the universal difference, which now asserts simply that all events are law-governed. This simple unity of law-likeness, however, is turned against any instance of a law, which must be the unification of the discreet moments of any event as the appearance of a stable rule. Their immediate unity is taken up as the law, but in the process, the difference is preserved as overcome. Only in the concept of the law itself, in the concept, that is, of universal difference, is the unity present as having overcome specific differences in this or that law described in purely conceptual, and simple or immediately unified, terms.[23]

With this pure concept, Hegel argues, we have returned to force, which now has the laws as its own. In the laws there are specific differences or determinations, but as law they are overcome, and as force, the many laws themselves are seen as a simple unity. But the very difference between force and its laws again disrupts the understanding's project, because the laws which belong to force express determinate differences to which force itself is indifferent. What we can see here is that the first claim made by the understanding, that what appears is really the law, has been superseded by the claim that the law governs what appears. While the former conception of the relation between law and appearance was plagued by the differences introduced by its emphasis on working from appearance to laws, the latter conception shows that beginning with the posited law-likeness of the appearances leaves any determinate expression of law-like behavior necessarily excluded by the simple unity of the law. If force is just that unity that must be behind all things, then no difference makes any sense, let alone finds its necessity in the law. No determinate law can defend either the necessity that there be such a law, that force be expressed in such a way, or the necessity that it be expressed in just these terms.[24]

The understanding is left with an ideal form of necessity to which its experience has driven it and the necessity that the ideal take on determinate forms, which it now posits as unnecessary. Remember that from the moment it took the concept of law to be its truth, the understanding was concerned to overcome differences in the name of a unity which preserved them abstractly, conceptually, as universal difference, the difference implicitly overcome in any universal term. We saw then that the developing experience of the understanding was itself cancelled and preserved only in the abstract by this unity that posits its own difference as overcome. What we can see here is that it has equally posited as overcome any difference whatsoever, and experiencing itself is a constant self-dissimulation, the appearance of universal, or overcome, difference. The differences of laws and force itself can be invoked in any explanation to restore the immediate or simple unity of experiencing. Any perceived situation or context is then immediately transposed into the inner world, but as the necessary simple unity of force. The truth of the understanding is that I *must* experience this field of determinate differences in order for it, the truth, to be true. With this "merely verbal" necessity, the understanding is plunged into crisis.

THE CRISIS OF THE UNDERSTANDING

There have been two constants guiding the experience of the understanding: the need to find the necessary unity of experiencing and the need to express this in objective terms, as the necessary unity of objectivity itself. In the crisis that follows the complete experience of the positing of the law as universal difference, the understanding consciousness is driven to see itself as the necessary unity of experiencing and to view its experiencing as a *self*-differentiating totality.

With the empty truth of the understanding's explanation that force must appear just like this, the project of making sense of the elements of perception has collapsed into tautology. The understanding at this point has to see that it has, on one level, advanced no further than saying that things and properties, or unities and differences, must be unified. To the extent that it has undergone a lengthy process of defining its project in terms which then had to be overcome, reintroducing old terms, and so on, the understanding finds itself lacking and senses its inability to get to the heart of things themselves.

For us, this is a direct consequence of the way the understanding turned what it discovered as the universal difference into a simple identity that is done with the differences it implies. The understanding turns to appearance with only a necessary unity over and above differences and then faces the task of identifying the appearance as unity. But having overcome all differences, its unity is indifferent to them, and the only way to explain appearance is either to invoke differences that just "show up," or that simply are, or to disregard them completely. As we have seen, in the former case, laws do not belong to force but to appearance itself, thus cannot carry the force of law. In the latter case, the understanding can say nothing beyond "it must be so." The understanding, in other words, can say no more of appearance than that it *is not* appearance, that is, it is not the unstable reflection of an inert law, but is either a reflection of something else, or not a reflection at all, but necessity itself. This is, in its simplest terms, the contradiction between what the understanding does and what it takes to be the truth of its activity.

What we can see then is that the relationship between law and appearance has to be one in which, as reflecting the differences the law comprehends, the appearance belongs to the law as its expression, as an appearance generated by and belonging to the law. There is no way to save the notion of appearance, or any meaningful notion of law, without reconciling them. As we saw with the universal difference, the law must give rise to certain appearances, appearances which can be understood only to the extent that they belong to the law on its own terms.[25]

For the understanding, which remains committed to a self-identical concept of unity, this can only mean another law, beside the law of force: the law of appearing itself.[26] According to this law, which the understanding, like perception, would take on as its own complication of a self-identical unity, unity is that which must generate differences which, as the differences of unity, belong to it and so return as overcome.

In stepping in for the understanding, we must remind ourselves that according to the law of force all differences are already overcome, thus the law of appearing and the law of force must be one. That is, the law requires its self-differentiation, it is the totality of self-differentiation as unified, and so force and appearing are aspects of one totality. This has the added consequence that the attempt to place the law of unity itself in objectivity, and the law of appearing in the understanding, is also a difference that must appear but which is equally overcome. Any difference between them is just another of our posited differences or a difference posited by experiencing itself.[27]

In refusing to allow the differences to be displaced onto different terms, we have been driven to recognize that what the experience of the understanding has been working with all along is a self-differentiating totality, one which makes distinctions within itself according to its own law. The law demands its own appearance, its own self-othering, in order to be the law that actually governs events. That this self-othering totality unifies the objective and the subjective, or is experiencing consciousness itself, means that consciousness per se, which takes its truth to be some determination of the objective sphere of experiencing, is itself overcome, and we are, as we have been, understanding the movement of consciousness itself; we are, that is, in the realm of self-consciousness.

Desiring Self-Consciousness

The transition that we have already marked from understanding consciousness to self-consciousness is shrouded in the text in the rather subtle language of the infinity of life, thus I want to describe what experiencing demands of us more clearly before showing why the language of life is appropriate here.

In the culminating moments of the experience of the understanding, two issues have taken shape as what that experience calls for in order to be comprehended. The first is that the unity we need to ascribe to appearing or experiencing is that of a self-differentiating totality; that is, a unity made up of differences it creates and resolves. The second is that this totality is experiencing itself, experiencing now understood as the unity not only of unity and difference, but also as the unity of self and other.

In the experience of desiring self-consciousness, we find the experiencing individual positing first an apparent difference between self and other, but as a difference that is not a difference, the *appearance* of the experiencing self as an other that finds its truth in its identity with the self. Like the understanding, desiring self-consciousness will learn that its very existence depends on its ability to respect appearance as an integral moment in the self-differentiating totality of consciousness.[28]

One of my primary concerns here is to mark the transformation of the straightforwardly epistemological preoccupations of the prior forms of conscious life into the context of living, desiring self-consciousness. It is a crucial transition for Hegel's argument and for my own, because it shows how the resistance demonstrated by *natural* consciousness toward life and determinate activity must be overcome in order to recover the truth object-oriented consciousness strives to achieve.[29] It is here, I will argue, that we learn why the truth sought by consciousness has to take the form of self-consciousness, and why it has to learn to be *inductive for-itself*. My analysis will be divided into three sections: (1) the concept of life as desire in-itself; (2) the relation between life as desire in-itself and natural consciousness; and (4) self-consciousness as desire for itself.

THE CONCEPT OF LIFE AS DESIRE IN-ITSELF

Hegel's chapter begins with a description of what has happened to the concept of the understanding as a result of the experience we have undergone. Simply put, we have recognized that the object we took to be something in-itself is in fact the movement of the concept deployed by consciousness, thus our concern here is to see how consciousness can have itself for an object, how it responds to its intrinsic self-differentiation.

Initially, it responds as the understanding does—namely, by seeking to cancel any "apparent" differences in the name of the overarching identity of experiencing consciousness. What is apparently other is really only the contents of its own experiencing, and so it seeks to cancel the differences within the experiencing consciousness (each and every difference which has emerged in it so far) and the difference between the experiencing consciousness and its experience in the name of the "I" it already is. In the "I," self-consciousness finds both its object and the agency by which the object is known.[30]

Notice, then, that the object of self-consciousness is the object of the various forms of consciousness we have already examined, but now understood as the dynamic of experiencing consciousness itself. The thing and its properties, for example, or force and its laws, are now seen as the expression of experiencing consciousness. There is no longer, in other words, any *real* difference within experiencing between the constitutive moments of those forms of conscious life, nor between the forms themselves as stages in the development we have seen. Experiencing *self*-consciousness takes these to be *immediately* its own differences, thus *is founded on excluding from its self-knowledge the role of its experiencing in generating those differences.*[31] Similarly, the difference between the experiencing itself and the "I" which claims it as its own is overcome, and so the active dynamic of experiencing is precluded from self-knowledge by the positing of a unity that asserts itself as the truth of all differences proper to experiencing itself. This unity that is achieved by the self's undoing the determinate differences of its object is the activity Hegel calls desire.[32]

But the object which it has at least tacitly recognized in positing itself as that object overcome is thereby a necessary moment in self-consciousness. The unity of experiencing self-consciousness presupposes and depends on as its object the appearance of experiencing consciousness, or experiencing in-itself.[33] The concept of *life* is that process of overcoming apparent otherness (or, again, un-self-conscious desire) which operates prereflectively, or in-itself but not for-itself; it is object-oriented consciousness understood now as the appearance of self-consciousness. If self-consciousness is the consciousness of the (need to overcome the) difference between self and apparent other, life is the consciousness of the other as to be overcome and the *implicit* determination that the other's truth is the living consciousness. That is, life is the desire which is unconscious of the fact that it is the unity in which differences are dissolved; or, it is unconscious of the unity it has posited between itself and its object.[34] It is the object, then, of the *need* for self-consciousness.

It is for this reason that life is the difference from self-consciousness necessitated by self-consciousness itself, the difference posited by the unity of self-conscious experiencing and cancelled therein. It is that which belongs to self-consciousness as the specific difference of its own self-differentiating totality, that is, that activity which is apparently not self-consciousness, or is self-consciousness awaiting self-confirmation. Life is a necessary moment in the coming-to-be of self-consciousness. The act in which self-consciousness asserts itself as the truth of an apparent other is the act in which it distinguishes itself from nonreflective self-consciousness, or life.

But notice that just as life is necessary to self-consciousness, its proper difference, so too is self-consciousness necessary for life to be recognized as itself, a recognition it is, by definition, incapable of developing. Let me examine in further detail life in the context of this incapacity for developing self-recognition.[35]

Self-consciousness emerges from the recognition that consciousness is a self-differentiating totality. According to the logic of self-differentiating totalities as it has developed to this point in our analysis, life must make differences within itself that are ultimately overcome. One such difference is the living being itself, which is set off from life as such as a determinate form of desire. Any individual living thing is defined as implicitly or unconsciously positing a specific object as what it requires for self-maintenance, or for life. It needs certain things to keep being the living thing it is, and this need is precisely the desire that defines it and its experience. To fall outside of the living thing's objective of self-maintenance is to be nothing; the only differences that matter are those which are the objects of its desire.

As we have already seen, the living being is not aware that it has posited its own conditions for self-maintenance as the truth of its experience, but it is aware of the need to react to those circumstances in which it is confronted by an apparently independent being whose independence is a threat to its posited objective. The behavior appropriate to each specific living individual is what it requires to overcome this apparent other; for example, to consume it. To satisfy its desire is both to provide for itself and, in the epistemological terms we have been working with, to confirm that it is the truth it has posited.

What we can see in its positing and consumption of those determinate others picked out by its desire is again a difference necessary to its being and necessarily cancelled in its being. The living thing posits its truth, its self-maintenance, as immediately the truth of its existence. All differences that fall within its self-maintenance, the things it desires as food, for example, are posited as really no difference at all.[36] They are uniformly regarded as its own food, and any particular details that might distinguish this food from that are of no significance, even if they require it to act in different ways. The living thing has as its truth a self-maintaining self-identity that is in no way mediated by otherness or by the experience of overcoming that other.

But it also is clear that the other is a difference that must be at least tacitly acknowledged, as to be overcome, and that the differences between beings to be overcome prescribe different forms of behavior.[37] To consume one kind of food might require lying in wait, or some kind of sophisticated performance, while others might require something different. For the living being itself, however, that which it claims to be the truth of is simply to be dissolved in the act of identification. So not only are its object's specific differences cancelled by the counter-assertion of the living thing that this is only an apparent difference, but the specific requirements for overcoming the apparent difference are equally cancelled in the move to confirm itself by destroying the object. In consuming, destroying, or dissolving the differences it experiences in order to realize itself as the immediate unity it (implicitly) posits, the living thing conceals its own being, the enacting of the logic of life which is defined by and expressed in its active relationship to the being of its objects, or in its *experiencing*. Life cannot develop self-recognition, or self-consciousness, because the activity it could become conscious of consists in dissolving and concealing the signs of its determinateness.

To the extent that any experienced difference makes a difference, it can only be by realizing the threat implicit in all meaningful difference: that the living being is not the truth of experience. The living being depends on overcoming all differences because any that persist challenge its posited claim. Every such challenge means life itself, and the only way difference could be allowed to persist would be if it overcame the living being. In serving as the food for another, for example, the living thing is itself dissolved. This is the key to the living thing's inability to recognize itself, or to develop a sense of itself as the unity of its experience. It is always faced with the dilemma of either dissolving all the differences that define it or being dissolved itself. Notice that either way it returns unconsciously to the overarching unity of life as such. It goes on living, bringing death to all its meaningful otherness, or it suffers death itself, and thereby shows (the conscious observer) that it was, in fact, only a living thing.

The movement of life as such is made up then of an indeterminate number of different exchanges, each of which results, as does their identity in life itself, in an *abstract* negation, the dissolution of differences in an abstract unity, or death.[38] Life itself is the unity of determinate acts and determinately related living beings continually dissolving themselves in death. Just as life is the difference necessary to the identity of self-consciousness, so too is death the difference necessary to the identity of life. And it is precisely because all life, all living, culminates in death, thus dissolving its specific differences, that it is incapable of developing self-recognition.

In its active self-dissolution, however, life mirrors the logic of what Hegel calls natural consciousness, and it is to this relation that I turn now.

LIFE AND NATURAL CONSCIOUSNESS

In examining Hegel's concept of life we have seen three ways in which its own activity amounts to a self-constructed barrier to developing self-consciousness: its unconscious positing of the appropriately determined objects, its unconscious positing of itself as the immediate unity of the appearance of those objects, and its execution or realization of that immediate identity in the consumption of its objects. This is, however, precisely the logic manifested by each of the forms of consciousness we already have examined. In what follows in this section, I will pursue this parallel to draw out of the term "natural consciousness" a more determinate logic than is often attributed it by the commentators to establish more clearly the relation between self-consciousness and what Hegel calls life.

In the introduction to the *Phenomenology of Spirit*, Hegel draws the reader's attention to the relationship between the development of conscious life projected by the text and that form of consciousness, *natural* consciousness, that is so burdened with its prejudices that it is "incapable of carrying out what it wants to undertake."[39] Natural consciousness is a persistent theme in the introduction; it is described as that which undergoes the process of developing a scientific standpoint,[40] but which is somehow intrinsically opposed to development and inclined to respond to the need for development by emphasizing the negative implications development has for what is already familiar.[41]

For those commentators who have noticed that natural consciousness is a determinate figure in the text's argument, its significance has been typically cast in terms of its lack of self-consciousness. Natural consciousness, like the consciousness of Husserl's life-world, is prereflective, thus the proper object of phenomenological analysis.[42]

But as the remarks cited above suggest, natural consciousness is not merely passive with respect to reflection, but an active obstacle.[43] As I argued in my last chapter, perceptual consciousness is the model of prereflective consciousness because the issue of just how the unity it posits actually organizes particular details is not yet thematized. Natural consciousness, on the contrary, *resists* thematizing and is an unlikely candidate for the kind of phenomenological development Hegel has in mind here because it refuses to submit its prejudices to analysis and it reads any call for development as a crippling rejection of the status quo.

This is just what we see in Hegel's description of each of the responses made by sensuous certainty, perception, and the understanding to the crises they have precipitated.[44] Indeed, the forms of consciousness, the shapes of conscious life which posit their truth as what is other than consciousness itself, are easily identified with natural consciousness if only because they share the realist's presupposition that the truth of experience has to be objective. But if we press further, what qualifies each of the forms of consciousness as natural holds equally for all the forms of conscious life whose experience is described in the *Phenomenology of Spirit*, with the exception, as I will argue later, of absolute knowing. This certainly seems to be what is implied in the remark in the introduction—that it is the path of natural consciousness "pressing forward to true knowledge" that the argument describes. To make this clearer, let me isolate what I take to be the logic appropriate to natural consciousness.

In each of the first three forms of consciousness, we have been able to identify a distinctive act of denial in the face of the difference between what each took to be the truth and what happens in trying to maintain that truth in concrete experience. The key to each rejection of experienced differences has been the immediacy, or *independence*, with which it identifies its truth, an immediacy that precludes any mediating agency on its part.

Self-proclaimed independence is the root of natural consciousness. When Hegel provides his general logic of consciousness in the introduction, he describes the differentiation of an object from consciousness, or what really is, and a way of relating that object back to consciousness that recognizes it as what is known. In each of the first three forms of consciousness, that relating has been precluded by the immediate form in which the initial distinction is made. For sensuous certainty, of course, there was no such initial difference, and we learned from it that this distinction, between what is and what is known, is necessary for experience to occur as a determinate relating of what has been distinguished. Both perception and the understanding recognized or posited versions of this distinction, the being of possible objects for knowing, as immediately self-relating: as properties to thing, or as appearances to laws.

Immediacy figures in each of these forms of consciousness in the same way it does in life: the posited other, or initial distinction, is posited as immediately related to itself, which *for* consciousness means itself *qua* object, and *in* life itself *qua* living thing. The determinate differences which mark the terms distinguished are immediately cancelled, or shown to be self-expressed, thus the behavior in which they are cancelled, or the *experience* each undergoes, is insignificant. What marks natural consciousness is what we saw in life: the exclusion from its awareness of the mediating activity that distinguishes it in the dissolution of its proper differences. While the object-orientation of consciousness is obviously a limit that is overcome, the more pressing concern once we reach self-consciousness is the continuing exclusion of the mediation, or *self*-mediation, of experiencing.

Consciousness is not identical then with natural consciousness but tends to pose as natural because the object-oriented truth it posits as immediately unified conceals the experiential mediation that is the origin of perceiving and understanding consciousness. In other words, natural logic is a function of *induction that remains concealed*, as its does in every shape of consciousness but one.[45] In fact, *natural logic is the 'problem of induction.'*

Natural consciousness *is* the problem of induction, the problem that belongs to induction, in two senses: first, because the inductive act of unifying experience, which constitutes each new form of conscious life, is concerned primarily with the moment of unity and has not yet learned to take responsibility for the differences belonging to that unity—it knows only incompletely, which is what it means to call it inductive in-itself; and second, because each act of unifying satisfies the current objective of inductive activity, to restore order to experiencing, consciousness becomes a tenacious defender of it over and against any differences that arise. But it *needs* to stake its life on what it has won if it is to undergo the kind of desperate crisis needed to initiate a new inductive development. It can only lose itself, or undergo "dismemberment," if holding fast to an immediately evident reality is all it has. In other words, the problem of induction is that it requires a sequence of stages of development, made up of several inadequate resolutions of differences, each of which *has* to be experienced as conclusive if it is to give rise to the truly disruptive crisis that serves the next stage. Natural consciousness is the claim that the unity is conclusive, thus both the 'natural' result of induction and the necessary condition for its continuing development.

The traditional problem of induction is an excellent example of a stage in the developing comprehension of experience that has succumbed to natural logic. The virtual stasis of traditional epistemology and its perpetual repetition of the debates surrounding realism, empirical science, and probability calculus, testify to the strength of the immediate dualism it has posited. Aside from its constitutive blindness to its own history, to the experiential ground of the necessity it posits in abstract categories, traditional epistemology is engaged in furiously repudiating the evidence that its project is in trouble. The translation of the problematic surrounding induction into the mathematical language of probability is the clearest indication of the determination of the adherents of abstract rationality to hold fast to their truth, no matter how many contradictions and inconsistencies it throws back at them. To claim that abstract reason is able to calculate and thus to bridge the opposition it has constructed between experienced multiplicities and its own categories is simply to bury the experience that ought to lead traditional epistemology out of its self-critical struggle. Induction is only problematic as a result of its refusal to identify its own struggle as the experience in question.

If the development we have already marked between these forms of consciousness is to occur it does so in spite of the natural posture consciousness tends to adopt. It is important to see as well that the development occurs, as we now know, because consciousness is really (if implicitly) self-consciousness or really (if implicitly) developing from experience. Natural self-consciousness ought to be an oxymoron, precisely because as self-consciousness it has already developed the recognition that consciousness is self-differentiating self-mediation.

That it isn't self-contradictory is suggested in the introduction, where one form of skepticism is defined as the "one-sided" interpretation natural consciousness gives to the discovery that it is the origin of experienced distinctions.[46] Once the logic of what is natural about consciousness is made clear, it shows up in every subsequent stage of the argument; observing reason and *Sittlichkeit*, for example, to the extent that each posits an immediate self-relation as the ultimate truth of an apparent difference, are forms of natural consciousness.

Desiring self-consciousness is natural to the extent that it posits the immediate cancellation of the differences between the forms of consciousness that serve as its origin, differences we can see are unified and distinguished as necessary stages in the development of experiencing. In the name of the self-relating certainty of the "I," the individual desiring or natural self-consciousness *immediately* identifies itself with the experiencing consciousness it is the truth of, *erasing the difference between its specific singular self and the self-determining totality of conscious life that is its object*. This is a contradiction of its own posited relation to consciousness, in which it is "the unity *for which* the infinite unity of the differences is."[47] Desiring self-consciousness shows itself to be another instance of abstract negation. I will turn now to the experience of this self-contradiction, the way in which it occurs for desiring self-consciousness.

DESIRE FOR-ITSELF AS NATURAL SELF-CONSCIOUSNESS

The first form of self-consciousness is desire for-itself, which exhibits the logic I have described as "natural" in positing the immediately self-relating identity of the "I."[48] In collapsing the differences generated in the development of experiencing consciousness, desiring self-consciousness betrays the logic of the self-differentiating totality with which it emerged from consciousness. For desiring self-consciousness, the determinate relationship of the understanding to self-consciousness is simply cancelled, thus desiring self-consciousness reveals its naturalness. It can only have conscious life, or experiencing, as its object by dissolving or killing it; like natural consciousness and life in general, death is its truth.[49]

Unlike life, however, in which the dissolution of determinateness concealed both the specific nature of the individual living thing and the fact that its behavior is informed by the logical principle of life, in natural or desiring self-consciousness the determinateness of the forms of experiencing are dissolved and its abstract power of negation is identified as *their* logical principle. In other words, natural self-consciousness posits the immediate truth of its singularity, as stripped of all determinate features, as the truth of the totality of conscious life. It replaces the determinate principles of the totality with the abstract principle of singularity. Desire, in this sense, makes sense of the world explicitly in terms of its own power of making sense of the world.

We have already examined, in the concept of life, what the object of self-consciousness ought to be in terms of its relationship to consciousness in a self-differentiating totality. What we need to examine now is how the natural consciousness experiences itself as self-defeating and what that experience provides for its inductive reconciliation.

As I have already noted, Hegel describes natural self-consciousness in the introduction as a kind of skepticism.[50] It gives up the object-oriented life of consciousness as a sham, an illusion dissolved in self-conscious negation. Skeptical or natural self-consciousness denies any intrinsic differences within its object and any development in the act in which it achieves it. Its life is the constant alternation of apparent objects and dissolving selfhood. Developing self-consciousness, Hegel argues, must instead be "the thorough-going skepticism" which identifies the determinate shapes of consciousness in the self-mediating, self-determining totality of experiencing selfhood.[51]

Desiring self-consciousness, like natural skepticism, is engaged in a constant alternation of apparent determinateness (the object it presupposes and is dependent on) and the cancellation of that determinateness in the act of identifying itself in an abstract negation. And like natural skepticism, desiring self-consciousness experiences the contradiction of its proclaimed independence. The immediate consumption of its object means that desiring self-consciousness is left with nothing to confirm its truth claim, no preserved testimony to its self-identity. Like any living thing, desiring self-consciousness finds that the limited satisfaction in consuming one object is quickly replaced by the need for another. It is frustrating its own desire to be the truth of all its experience by destroying any independent expression of itself. Just to be self-consciousness, it requires the appearance of independence; like the understanding, its defeats its own endeavor if it cheats that appearance of its relative independence.[52]

In its unrequited desire for another that reflects it as its truth, desiring self-consciousness experiences its dependence on its object as *need*, the need that produces the object that is the truth of desire: a self-differentiating in which what is other, experiencing consciousness, *necessarily* belongs.[53] And if its truth is not immediate and so determined in advance as unified, self-consciousness must give up its desire and recognize its object, or experiencing, as mediating its truth, or as *self*-mediating.

But the recognition that it needs its other, that it depends on it, is incomplete if it stops here. To be the truth of experiencing consciousness, self-consciousness needs to show that it is the truth of this object. But to be this truth immediately, or to determine it as complete in advance, is as we have seen to cancel or dissolve that of which it is the truth. Immediacy, in other words, affects not only the *form* of its truth relation, but its *content* as well. To give up its claim of immediacy, self-consciousness has to recognize that its object mediates the content of what it will claim as its truth.

What self-consciousness needs, therefore, is to investigate the other, to see how its truth is expressed in experiencing itself. It must, in other words, approach experiencing consciousness or conscious life as an independent, self-determining totality that is in its movement the expression of the truth of selfhood.[54] To be self-conscious *is* to have the movement of experiencing that is in-itself, for-itself. If it merely posits itself as that truth, it is no different from the in-itself, or conscious life, because *its own movement means nothing to it.* To be self-conscious is to have learned from experiencing what it is, to preserve its differences as the self-mediation conscious life cannot comprehend. To be self-conscious, then, is to be the truth mediated by, or learned from, experiencing. Self-consciousness *must be inductive.*

For the singular self of desiring self-consciousness, this means that it must learn to be *inductive for-itself.* It must *learn to learn from experiencing* how it is the truth of experiencing. If it is to salvage its own project and throw off the logic of natural self-consciousness, it must give up the immediacy it posits, the immediacy of its singularity, and embrace its dependence on what experience shows it. As we will see, it must become a slave to its experience to learn inductively how it can become its truth.

But the contradiction it experiences as the unfulfilled desire for self-identification is not sufficient to dislodge the natural logic of desire. Being natural, it refuses to admit the self-defeating logic of its experiencing. What is required is that its experienced other claim its independence for itself and explicitly challenge the posited immediacy of the desiring self-consciousness. Insofar as its object is conscious life, which is in-itself but not for-itself, that cannot happen.

What it requires then is an advocate for the independence of its experienced object, another being for-itself. It needs another being that posits its independence, another desiring, or (merely) living or natural self-consciousness.[55] Only then will the apparent threat to its immediacy fight for itself, assert its own independence at all costs, and force desiring self-consciousness to learn to recognize its dependence on life.

Conclusion

In this chapter, I have described the attempts to secure the truth of conscious life by reflecting on its unity. From the experience of the understanding, we learned that the unity of conscious life cannot be abstracted from its differences, but must recognize them as moments in a self-differentiating totality. Such a totality must both generate and recover its own specific differences. We also learned that this self-differentiating totality of experiencing consciousness is nothing other than consciousness itself, or what we called desiring self-consciousness.

In the experience of desiring self-consciousness, the individual self immediately identifies itself as the truth of experiencing. It cancels the differences between the unity of its particular self-conscious singularity and the different forms of experiencing the stages in the development of the logical principle of experiencing consciousness, or conscious life, that are its object. What we learned here was that to be the truth of experiencing consciousness, it has to investigate experiencing on its own terms, and overcome the natural logic of immediate self-identity. As a self-*differentiating* totality, it has to learn to recognize those differences in conscious life as self-*mediating*. That is, it has to learn that its identity is something that depends on the experiencing it claims to be the truth of. Finally, we saw that it has to become inductive for-itself in its attempt to show itself to be the truth of experiencing; it can only be the truth of experiencing insofar as it has learned from it how it demands to be unified. It must recognize the self-mediating status of forms of experiencing, then, in an act of self-comprehending. Finally, we learned that only an other being for-itself, an other desiring self-consciousness, can provide the disruption of the first self-consciousness' posited immediacy necessary to initiate its education.

Now I turn to that inductive self-education itself in which the individual self will learn from experiencing its place in the self-determining totality of experiencing consciousness.

CHAPTER THREE

Induction and the Experience of the Singular Self

Introduction

In the previous chapter, we learned that selfhood is the truth of what happens in conscious life, and that this truth must take the form of an inductive reflection on the determinate ways that conscious life mediates the truth of selfhood in its experiencing. To fulfil this, we saw, required that the reflecting self learn to recognize the self-determining nature of conscious life, and it is to the inception of that education that I turn now in examining the section of Hegel's text entitled "The Independence and Dependence of Self-Consciousness."

In pursuing the nature of conscious life, the self faces two hurdles: the need to come to terms with its dependence on conscious life—the object of self-consciousness—and the need to come to terms with the threat to its claim to be the truth of conscious life—an other self-consciousness, an other that is experienced as for-itself. I will be first concerned with establishing how the self, which has already ceded its primacy to that of the other desiring self-consciousness (or which is self-enslaved), is able to learn about itself from being driven to become attentive to its own experience. That is, I will look at the experience of the enslaved self as one in which it becomes, for the first time, *inductive for-itself.*

In the two later sections of this chapter I will describe how the slave's inductive openness is conditioned by the institution of slavery and by the developing concept of experience, in ways which conceal them from the slave. The first of these will address the role of the institution the self enters in its becoming inductive. The second will examine the ongoing experience of consciousness, connecting the experience of slavery to the experience of desiring self-consciousness to point to the broader context informing the experience of slavery and its necessary exclusion from the slave's act of inductive self-consciousness. My goal in altering the sequence prescribed by Hegel's analysis is to emphasize the hierarchy of contexts as they become an object of inductive self-consciousness and to prefigure the subsequent stages in its inductive education. From these perspectives, I will describe how, by entering into the institution, the slave-self provides the experience to ground an initial induction and brings to life the structure that will serve as the object of a subsequent induction, culminating in the inductive recognition of the unity of the concept of experience.

The Experience of the Life of Slavery

Accounts of this section of the *Phenomenology of Spirit* are as varied and even opposed as those of perhaps any other section. I will be concerned here with a reading that is suggested, even if only tacitly, by a number of commentators but which has been made explicit in my research only in John Russon's *Hegel on the Body*. Russon identifies the slave, in part, as concerned first and foremost with developing the requisite skills for carrying out its duties—Russon argues, then, that the story of the slave is an important account of education, and that this educational element is of prime importance in this section of the work. For Russon, the slave learns through developing an appropriate approach to mediating the master's desire, an education which culminates in learning about itself as a mediator. I will address how learning that one is a mediator—a formative influence on the world—is itself the result of having one's mediating mediated in turn by experience. I will develop a parallel account of the way in which induction turns out to look very much like education, which, if my description of induction as "learning from experience" is true, should not be surprising.[1]

In Hegel's analysis, the life of the slave-self is one in which it is initiated into a regimen built around working upon the natural world to satisfy the desire of the master. My goal in this section is to show how the process of initiation depends upon the slave's ability to become inductive, to learn from its experience with the material of its labor to recognize a determinate aspect of the selfhood that made it possible.[2]

The life of the slave is governed primarily by the imperative of compelled service. The slave-self's existence is organized by its need to satisfy the will of the master, whose authority the slave has identified as its own. Carrying out that will, however, demands of the slave a more complex relationship to its world than is necessarily recognized in executing its responsibilities, and it is through this complexity that the experience of the slave prepares self-consciousness for further development.

The slave has to mediate between the master's will and the world from which the means to satisfy it are to be drawn. In asking "How can I serve?" the slave is implicitly asking "How am I constrained to respond to the world?" No matter how determinate the orders are from the master's side (harvest the grapes, clean the stables), they take the form of goals to be realized, and it is the slave's responsibility to uncover the appropriate method for their realization.

But the slave is by no means independent; the slave's life is one of service, which is to say continuously motivated and informed by the master. This constant presence takes the form of the alternative at the very center of the slave's being: work or perish. The threat of death, the legacy of the logical origins of slavery in the life-and-death struggle,[3] is both constant and pervasive. The slave's labor is literally work against death.

The fear that drives the slave in its work has three notable features: its pervasiveness, persistence, and indeterminacy. In its pervasiveness, it binds every aspect of the slave's life to the will of the master—there is no place in the slave's existence where that fear is dispelled and no task that doesn't bear death as a possible outcome. The fear is equally persistent—no amount of work or success overcomes the threat of death, and the slave's life is as temporally bound to the master's will as it is spatially. Indeed, it is through shattering the ordinarily self-imposed limits on time and space that the master's threat of death becomes truly indeterminate—there is nothing that can shield the slave from the master's control over its life. In this indeterminacy of fear, in its being more than a threat and actually something that inspires an all-consuming dread, the slave experiences a master that transcends the personality of its human ruler.[4] This is a crucial component of the slave's emerging selfhood: what ultimately drives its action is *fear for its own life*. Its work in transforming the natural world is something that will express the extent to which that life makes a difference in self-preservation.

Fear is not a source of paralysis, however, but an impetus to work.[5] And if the slave can never work off the threat of death it can work it down. This means, initially, that the slave must plunge into labor, doing whatever it takes to satisfy the master's commands. Part of what this involves is another attempt at overcoming the conceptual legacy of consciousness: its reverence for the natural existence of the objective world.[6] The combination of fear and the need to work on nature to stave off death necessitates the subordination of the natural to the life of the slave and the transformation of the natural from an independent being to the material for effecting the slave's survival.

At the same time, the slave is forced to recognize in the natural world a kind of independence. To the extent that its orders require it to use the natural world to serve the desire of the master, the slave is forced to recognize that the natural world carries within it certain limits, certain prescriptions for how it is to be manipulated. Reckless harvesting or fertilization destroys the productivity on which the slave's life depends, thus in its work the slave is driven to come to terms with the determinate features of the various forms of natural life it encounters. The concrete acts which comprise the slave's labor involve both the determination of the natural world as that which serves the slave's self-preservation and the readiness to accept the corresponding demands imposed by the specific objects of its labor.

This leads to a second modification of the slave's implicit question. Instead of asking "How am I constrained (by the master's orders) to deal with the world?" the slave must ask "How does the world insist that I treat it in transforming it in the name of my survival?" It is in this primitively scientific outlook that the experience of slavery begins.[7]

The problem facing the slave now is the fact that there is no immediate solution to this question. Regardless of the slave's position within the master's estate (the very first slave, or the latest in generations of slaves), the precise set of prescriptions imposed by the forms of natural life it has to deal with can only be uncovered for *this* slave, over time. Harvesting or planting one plant now doesn't guarantee that another won't be killed by untimely intervention, a result that cannot be anything but disastrous for the slave. The combined forces of fear, labor, and the determinate forms of natural life put the slave in a position where it has to learn how best to mediate the master's desire and the material for its satisfaction. It is in this necessary process of education that the slave is forced to become inductive—that is, to learn from experience how to achieve the desired results.

The course of the slave's education is inductive, first because in setting to work on an initially alien set of material, the slave is driven to revise again the implicitly interrogative approach it takes to the world. The initial efforts to bring about the master's desired state of affairs runs up against the slave's lack of familiarity with the relevant technique. In producing what the master wants, the slave is required to meet specific standards other than its own. Meeting them is not something the slave can accomplish immediately; rather, it must set those standards as the goal and be prepared for a series of attempts, each of which brings it closer to realization. The slave's question is now "What does my experience of dealing with the world tell me I have to do to bring it in line with my project of self-preservation?" The slave must repeatedly examine its own formative involvement with the natural world to gauge the success or failure of its particular method of bringing about the master's desired end.

In the language of traditional epistemology, the slave's experience is inductive precisely because each and every encounter with its experienced other is made meaningful because it reads from the particular thing it is involved with, toward an understanding of its labor in a manner dictated by its experiencing itself.[8] It sees not some particular lump of earth but the field that will yield grain. The entire world of the slave is informed and determined by an authoritative or universal self, the threatening master. By ordering its experience of the world according to this authority, the slave animates its world meaningfully.

But the traditional language of epistemology doesn't do justice to the transformative sense of induction I have argued organizes Hegel's account.[9] In evaluating its performance and results, the slave is concerned to *improve* its success in manipulating the material conditions of its own survival. The initial efforts, which depend on positing the way the natural world gives itself to be consumed, have to be revised in light of what that labor shows as the difference between success and failure. The goal must be to 'get to the bottom of things,' to find what form of intervention the natural world demands. The key to realizing this goal is the preparatory nature of the slave's labor: while the master's desire seeks the consumption and destruction of what the slave produces, the slave itself is engaged in building up what is to be consumed. Its approach must be constructive. With each renewed assault on the natural world, the slave forms and reforms what is to be its offering to the master. Because the slave's task requires that it effect change on the world, the results of its efforts are the measure of success, and they must be *read* in precisely those terms. The slave must become (primitively and implicitly) scientific, treating every stage of its work on the natural world as indicative of some larger truth, the resolution of the master's desire.

This in turn requires that the slave view the outcome of each specific move in terms of its having contributed to building up the object commanded by the master. Each failure and each limited success is made meaningful only to the extent that it brings the slave nearer to (or takes it further from) the projected result. With each new insight some new way of making the material over is made possible, and the slave must put it to work. The presence of the master's threat forces the slave to practice induction, or development by determinate negation, as I described in the first chapter.

In calling the slave's experience inductive I am describing the relationship between a universal principle, here in the form of the selfhood of the master whose authority the slave has recognized, and its work in transforming versions of this principle from the force of necessity to the necessary expression of the natural world. The slave is required to bring the world to reflect the master's desire, and its experience is always of the *difference* between posited goal and present reality. Because the slave lives by actively unifying the two, it is required to build out of the natural world its implicit reflection of the master's self, or desire. Unlike the forms of consciousness we already have experienced, the slave's life is *defined* as mediation, as mediating the determinateness it encounters and the principle it must find within the determinateness, and it is as the singular moment in mediation that it will be able to find itself. The slave's experience cannot rest on propping up a contradictory or self-defeating approach to experience; rather, the slave depends on its ability to recognize failure and transform its approach accordingly. Because death now has been recognized as an objective threat, and one which hangs on some ultimate failure, the revision of one's strategies is the very fight against death. There is for the slave no either/or in its fear of death—it has decided against death and will do everything in its power to realize its decision.

Induction, or learning from experience, occurs for the slave in three distinct moments. First, the slave interprets its surroundings in terms of their adequacy as objects for the master. Whatever gap exists between the way things are and the way they ought to be is then bridged by the slave's work, work which has as its objective making up the difference between expectation and the way things presently appear. The task of bringing what is up to the master's standard is mediated, however, by the limits prescribed by the natural material at the slave's disposal, thus it must learn from the outcome of the initial attempt what gulf remains and, more importantly, what that outcome tells it about what is to be done to overcome it. It is driven, then, to read the natural world which exists as its other, as the *appearance* of the master's will. In the second moment, these results are interpreted by the slave as objectives, not merely for what nature requires but of what is required of it to get the job done. It is important to see that the third moment, in which the slave reapplies itself to the task of transforming the natural world, is not the abstractly inductive appraisal of what the slave *thinks* is the answer to its problem, but the urgent assessment of what must be done next, given what has turned up in the wake of the last approach, to get the thing right and save one's life.[10]

In this way, the slave's inductive labor literally builds up a more successful *engagement* with the natural world. As we saw in the analysis of desiring self-consciousness, abstract reflection repels self-consciousness from conscious life, the very in-itself that it must have as its object. Serving the master, the slave is initially focused precisely on what it is doing and has done. *Over time*, the slave uncovers the conditions for successful involvement with or mediation of the world, learning from what it has done what must be done next to bridge the gap between what does not yet and what will please the master.

But the experience of slavery is not an education in horticulture; it is, as Hegel reminds us, an experience of self-consciousness.[11] The slave's inductive demands on the natural world are expressed not merely in an increasingly fruitful outcome but more significantly in an awakening sense of increasingly proficient management of its material—which material now must include the results of its own work on and with the natural world. We saw in the progress of consciousness (from sensuous certainty to understanding and desiring self-consciousness) ever more appropriate responses to the experience of the demands of cognition, but also an inability to recognize the role of the self in enacting the mediating principle of experiencing. In the experience of slavery, the slave is able to find in its work evidence of the success of its attempts to bring about the master's wishes—that is, in becoming self-consciously inductive, it is able to become self-conscious, inductively. I will now more closely examine this.

Remember that the extent of the slave's fear served to invade and break down its sense of time and space; in reclaiming these through fear, the master is able to destroy completely the customary sense of the world the slave may have had. Every aspect of the slave's existence is now wrapped in fear, and work provides the only way for it to assert itself by reflecting that fear.

As such, the slave's work represents a singular goal adopted in the name of self-preservation.[12] The natural world upon which it works, as I argued above, becomes the material of that self-preservation, and through its labor is increasingly divested of its apparently independent being. But (and this is to say the same thing) the slave's material has to include its work and its results, and the natural world is now interpreted in terms of that work and those results.

The slave, then, *becomes its own 'other,'* as with each new effort at forming the natural world the slave's evaluation of the experience of past attempts makes its work, and not an unformed world, its object.[13] This is the thrust of the slave's *transformative* induction: it is not passively recording or abstracting from its experience but building a world that increasingly conforms to the imperative ordering its labor. While the explicit focus for the slave must remain, ultimately, the master's desire, it comes to inhabit and experience a world made familiar, a world already stamped with the slave's history of intervention. The culmination of the slave's work then is not a natural world that has given up its secrets but the result of a series of enforced transformations, a thing *made* by the slave. To the extent that it succeeds in satisfying the master, the natural world *is* what the slave has made of it to stave off death.

The slave's inductive attitude toward the natural world then involves taking up its experience in terms of its ability to have transformed it from what resists it in meeting the master's desire, to the finished product that provides for the master's satisfaction. To make this thing for the master means its life, and all of its energy must be devoted to solving this 'problem of induction.' If as work the slave's experience is objectified, making this inductive development possible, it is through fear and its forcing the slave to be attentive to the way that the natural world responds that its experience attains an *independence* while remaining at the same time essentially its own.[14]

In the discussion of desire,[15] I argued that self-consciousness, in the freedom of its reflective act, had to respect the integrity of its own conscious life. The slave's fear of the master and the necessity of working to fight it off makes this respect possible. It is, however, as the slave satisfies the master's will that this respect is able to be transformed into an act of self-consciousness. The results of the slave's labor bear a sense not only of what the slave has staked (life itself) on success but also of the history of its coming to meet the master's standards. They are a determinate expression of the slave's ability to come to terms with the conditions for survival. The slave has formed the world on its own,[16] and neither its subsequent consumption by the master nor its independence can undo what the slave has been able to do in producing it. What endures then is not the object for the master but the sense of self it has brought the slave.

The slave's inductive approach to its labor is the *means* by which the slave builds up the determinate expression of selfhood, the *object* of the culminating act of self-consciousness, and the *method*[17] used to enact self-consciousness. I will address the contents of this act, and what it excludes, before taking the latter up in more detail in the next two sections.

What the slave learns of itself in reflecting on the finished work is that it is the difference that made a difference, the singular determinate self filling in a world framed by fear. As Hegel notes, the slave's sense of self is not ultimately shaped by the role it has taken in the master's estate but by the abstract negativity of death.[18] It is in the name of its own life, stripped bare by an all-consuming fear, that the slave works, and it is the singular, vital self that emerges in fashioning the master's object. It is this living, world-transforming being[19] that the slave comes to see in its product.

In taking the constructed object of the master's desire as a determinate expression of its own selfhood, the slave has rightly fixed its gaze on its experience. As the dialectic of desire demonstrated, recognizing conscious life as an independent or self-determining whole was the key to self-conscious selfhood, and this is what the slave accomplishes. The terms of this whole, or totality, include for the slave the experience it has brought about as a singular self, the principle ordering its development (the fear of the master, or the fear for its own life), and the resulting context (the transformed natural world, and specifically the object it presents to the master). The slave is able to take as an object not only an expression of the way that living consciousness forms and responds to its world for its own sake, but also, because of its history of being revised in accordance with its own need to meet specific demands, an expression with which the slave identifies its own unique existence.

Calling the slave's self-conscious approach to its work inductive and the culminating reflection on the finished product inductive means seeing that for the slave what is before it is the result of a *history* of its own experience.[20] The slave's sense of self is grounded in recognizing that 'this work before me is what *I have done* in responding to the conditions for my survival.' The slave's reflection satisfies the conditions worked out in the analysis of desire because it depends upon it recognizing, in its work, what we can call the self-determining totality of its experiencing consciousness. It reflects on a determinate aspect of its experience, its product, and sees it as an expression of its ongoing involvement with the natural world. Its reflection is mediated or limited by, or better yet *dependent on* its active engagement with the natural world over time. It sees itself as the *singular* center of this totality, not only in terms of its ability to organize it to the slave's own (which is to say the master's) satisfaction but also precisely as someone who *achieved* this centrality by meeting the conditions of its experience.

However inflated its sense of self may have been to begin with, it is only because it was forced to surrender that merely posited sense to the conditions of its experience, to its concrete acts of labor, that it wins it back in real terms.[21] The product that satisfies the master alone constitutes the slave's victory, and its realization is simultaneously its own realization as a singular self-consciousness.

To characterize its act of self-consciousness as inductive then is again to emphasize its sense of self as having been actualized or worked out in and from its experience over time. It is to the extent that its newly forged selfhood emerges in, triumphs over, and is reflected by its experience that it sees what it could not have seen before. Its own history belongs to and authorizes its selfhood. Selfhood, for the slave, is real because it is grasped retrospectively, *inductively*, as what its experience of responding to the conditions for its survival have produced. Moreover, it has identified with its inductive singularity, its capacity for realizing a unified and organized totality from an experienced multiplicity.

The slave's lesson in selfhood remains, however, from the standpoint of the education of the desiring self-consciousness, incomplete. There are two further dimensions to its experience still necessarily concealed. In the sections that follow, I will examine these in more detail to see how the conditions that enforce their concealment drive the slave's education beyond the boundaries of slavery.

The Experience of the Institution of Slavery

In the first section, we have seen how the enslavement of the experiencing individual has enabled it to become self-consciously inductive and inductively self-conscious—that is, the slave-self has learned from its experience that its conscious life includes the capacity to respond to its experience of determinate or particular differences by organizing or unifying them, or, to learn from experience.

In this section, I will examine the role of the institution in making the slave's initiation into selfhood possible. I will argue that it is *as* an institutionally defined role that slavery enables the kind of developed relationship to one's singularity we have seen in the first section.

With the term *institution*, I am describing slavery as an intersubjective totality that is organized as the principled relationship between a *universal* or sanctioning form of selfhood, which claims to stand as the truth of the experience of its individual members and the members themselves.[22] An institution is, as the name suggests, a self-conscious construct, something instituted by experiencing individuals as a way of recognizing both the intrinsically social implications of self-consciousness and its *unnaturalness*—that self-consciousness doesn't just happen but is the result of a reflection on the experience of being with others. The institution is the way in which the lesson learned by desiring self-consciousness, that its truth had to be recognized as the truth of an other self-consciousness, is incorporated into conscious life.

Slavery fails, in a number of tragic ways, to meet even the most minimal standards of institutional logic. Remember that at the end of the last chapter we saw that desiring self-consciousness needed to have its object reflect independently that the desiring self was its truth, and that the only kind of being able to reflect selfhood as its truth was another self-consciousness. I suggested that any project of realizing self-consciousness was then necessarily social and in some sense *consensual*: the other self had to actually identify as the truth of its experience what the first self had identified.

The institution of slavery is certainly not consensual. One of the reasons it will undergo its unique crisis is because although it *is* built on consensus, that is, the slave has to agree to do the master's work and to recognize the master as the truth of its selfhood, the master insists that it is not, and that the slave isn't even the kind of being (a real self) that could consent to any agreement at all. For the master, the slave is just an extension of the master's own being, a tool or implement needed to facilitate the master's desires.

But this is not to say that it isn't an institution. Rather, it is an institution that isn't yet self-conscious and which needs to undergo some form of development to bring the recognized roles it has presupposed into the open. In this respect, it is not so different from the institutions we will examine in the next chapter, which also deny some essential moment of institutional logic.

In this section, I will examine the ways in which the slave's selfhood, the very singularity it uncovers in its labor, is already determined by the institutional role of slavery and its relation to the role of the master and so is a product of the institution. My goal is to identify the institutional relationship between master and slave as a necessary element of the slave's selfhood in order to draw out the extent to which its project of self-consciousness is incompletely realized in the vital singularity emphasized in the previous section.

It should be clear that the roles played in the slave's development by fear and labor indicate a more sophisticated totality than the merely natural concerns for self-preservation the slave is able to recognize. Fear and labor are commanded by the self whom the slave has recognized, in entering the institution, as its truth. They are the ways in which the slave relates to its own posited *universality*. I will examine each separately.

The master organizes the institution according to the logic of desiring self-consciousness, in which all relations are governed by or culminate in death. We have already described the role of fear in breaking down the slave's 'natural' identity. The slave, who has (as we will see in the next section) already granted the master authority over life and death, is reduced by the pervasive nature of the threat to a being focused solely on survival. This is precisely what we would expect of an institution based on desire, because the slave is what is merely living, thus the apparent object of the master's authority. Because the master's universal selfhood is cast in terms of an indeterminate fear, the master is not a determinate reflection of the slave's selfhood but the repeated threat that the master could at any time desire the slave's death. The slave has recognized as the truth of its experience the power of life and death.

In living, however, the slave is not merely the positive being I described. The slave is put to work for the master, and the constant threat of death means that the slave must approach its labor on the natural world with a reflective respect for its integrity that is missing in merely vital relations. The slave isn't just this or that desiring being, but one beholden to what it has already granted absolute authority. It is in virtue of its institutional status, its relation to another higher self, then, that the slave is already more than merely living. Let me pursue the relation between the master and slave in terms of the institutional potential for self-development.

Remember that the experiencing self-consciousness who is entering slavery is in no specific way prepared for the tasks prescribed by the master. What qualifies it to enter slavery is nothing more than the recognition of the master as the truth of its experience and its recognition that its life means more to it than death. Once within slavery, however, the selfhood of the master personifies both the threat of death and the demand for work. The life of the slave is institutional and already a form of self-consciousness in the limited sense that it has identified itself as its own authority, a universal authority in the form of a relation to another self, and has that authority brought to bear on it in the form of fear and the need for labor.

The slave's labor begins with a prescribed and determinate objective. The slave identifies itself with this objective as the goal not only for guaranteeing its survival but also (and this is the same thing, because the principle of life is animating the truth of the master self for the slave) for reconciling itself with its truth, for living up to the conditions imposed by its self-consciousness. That is, as the life of self-consciousness, the slave has to regulate its behavior in accordance with the presence of the universal or authorizing selfhood of the master. In learning how to be a slave, the slave is learning how to be subject to its own truth. Slavery is an overarching project of self-realization, mediated by the concrete desire of the master.

The labor of self-realization is the first step out of the logic of natural consciousness. The wholly positive and immediate claims made by natural consciousness were not able to tolerate or admit mediation or realization. They were a set prescription for experience and unable to be developed or renegotiated in light of any experienced difficulties. The singular living consciousness recognized no other authority than what it posited.[23]

In identifying itself with an objective, however, the experiencing individual has incorporated the necessity of responding to any experienced inadequacies in its project, and it has identified as its goal an other selfhood whose universality it is in the process of realizing and which therefore survives any errors or miscues. That is, unlike the merely living thing for whom contradiction meant death, the slave is not yet identified with its universal principle and has to work out a set of material conditions before it can satisfy the universal. Rather than perishing through failure to realize its objectives, the slave has death as a threat, as something it can anticipate and prevent, thus it can learn to suffer changes to its provisional plan for organizing its experience of the natural world. It is precisely because the slave has identified itself with *a project* defined by the universal (or institutionally defining) self and already become more than the merely living singularity that it comes to recognize as itself that the slave makes experientially mediated or inductive development possible, and the possible *object* of the inductive reflection on singular selfhood.[24]

It is in having to work, in being required to execute this potential for self-development, that the slave's emerging selfhood is actualized by the institution. There are three ways in which the slave's labor builds from the energy of its own singularity a determinate expression of the master's, or its own, universality. The first of these comes from the specific demands of the master. While the universal fear of the master strips from the slave any domain it could call its own, any space or time proper to it, the nature of the master's demand for service specifies instead work appropriate to a single living productive force. The slave doesn't choose or happen upon the tasks it is to perform. They are defined by the master's desire, and what the tasks define in turn is a singular set of objectives. The key to the slave's subsequent sense of itself as a living, singular, experiencing center is the master's precluding any positive trace of selfhood (family, personality, etc.) through fear and the reinscription of a limited number of purely productive goals. The slave, to the extent that it has really faced the fear of death, sees even what we might call "teamwork," solely in terms of its own potential death, thus in terms of its own specific task. It is in relation to the master, then, that the slave is reduced to a single living force.[25]

Second, the slave's work, that which provides the context and object of its transformative induction leading to the recognition of selfhood, is more primordially organized by the need to be recognized as satisfying the master, as providing for the master's desire. It is the master who wants something done, made, produced, and it is to the master's gaze that the slave's work must be subjected. In its work, the slave has identified its own survival with the production of the master's desired object, and so it is as the desiring master, or the universal self, that the slave scrutinizes the results of its labor. Setting to work actualizes the identification between the slave and its universal that is implicitly posited in agreeing to serve as a slave. The slave actually represents the will of the master in mediating its relationship to the natural world. It is because the slave stands in as it were for the master in evaluating its own work in preparation for submitting it to the master that its work becomes productive in terms of its own self-consciousness at all.[26]

Finally, the slave's culminating reflection, the moment in which selfhood in its limited sense is defined for it, is conditioned by its having met with the master's approval. It is *because* it satisfied the master that it can stand as testimony to the power of its living selfhood. Granting this approval is the master's defining act, the confirmation that the master is the truth of this productive experience, and the slave's reflection on self-hood is then inseparable from, and dependent upon, the act of the master. But as the defining act of the master, it is more profoundly the *denial* of the slave's selfhood. Before turning to this tension in the institution of slavery, let me summarize the ways in which the institution determines implicitly the slave's selfhood.

By internalizing the self whose authority the slave lives by confirming, the slave is able to recover its own selfhood as having lived up to this authority. The slave-self must face the conditions of conscious life explicitly, in the life of the slave to the master. The master spells out what must be done, what will count as having done it, and determines when it has truly been accomplished. What sets the slave's experience apart from the master's is its need to internalize the merely posited authority of the master, to take it over as defining its experience, defining the whole of its productive working relations with the natural world. Crucially, in learning to become a slave for a master,[27] the slave makes explicit the range of its singular experiencing, from confronting a world only abstractly defined in its own terms (i.e., as not meeting the objective that its life depends on) to a world that in determinate ways has come to be realized as truly its own (as one in conformity with the master's will) by the mediating role of its experiencing singularity.

But the dependence of the slave's sense of selfhood on the institutional life under the master is concealed for the slave, whose selfhood is determined as vital and productive, as singular and not as intersubjective or institutional. The reason for this lies in the master's refusal to recognize the productive experience that has yielded its desired object as a self. Just as the master, and the institution of slavery that sanctions both the nature of the master and the nature of the slave, belongs to and makes possible the slave's self-consciousness, it restricts it in a manner that has a decisive impact on the institution and all those shaped by it.

Because the confirmation of the slave's success in its work takes the form of the master's consumption of the results, the slave can only discover itself to the extent that it can reclaim it in some sense from the master. The very act of mastery involves taking on the selfhood of the slave, and every act of consumption reinforces that refusal to let the slave's declaration of intrinsic selfhood become an explicit feature of the institution. Just as in the logic of desiring self-consciousness we saw its simultaneous dependence on and dissolution of the determinate forms of implicit selfhood or life, the institution of slavery sanctions the master's immediate self-satisfaction through denying the mediation of the slave. The master, like desiring self-consciousness, is defined in immediate opposition to experiencing. The institution that defines the master as the truth of the slave's selfhood is founded on denying the slave's selfhood in any form. Not only then does the (institutional) experience of becoming a slave not enter the slave's act of self-consciousness, because the master's presence as fear drives it to reassert itself in terms of the life under the threat of death; so long as it is a slave, it can never explicitly proclaim its selfhood even as the living singularity that makes the master's satisfaction a reality. But the slave has already worked out the conditions for recognizing its selfhood, and the master, and the institution as a whole, is unstable precisely because it demands that the material conditions of institutional selfhood be worked out, or elaborated, and then immediately denies that this is the truth of its own prescriptions.

If any act of declaring selfhood is equally an act of asserting mastery, the slave cannot *qua* slave continue the induction it began. What it needs, in other words, is to find some way of effecting its selfhood by adopting a degree of "mastery" that effectively transforms its role from slave to independent self. This transformation, in which the slave identifies itself as what Hegel calls a stoic, occurs necessarily beyond the institution of slavery, and does not, cannot, include that institution as an aspect of its selfhood, precisely because to the extent that it belongs to it the slave-self is defined by the master whose authority it recognizes as merely living and incapable of selfhood.[28]

I turn now to the third dimension of the slave's experience, the conceptual history of consciousness, in order to examine how the necessity of institutional selfhood arises.

The Experience of Slavery

We have seen how the preliminary inductive reflection on the nature of selfhood depends on a series of concrete encounters with an other that is not self-conscious (the natural world upon which the slave works), and how these encounters are informed by a series of contemporaneous encounters with an other whose self-consciousness prohibited the fulfillment of the inductive reflection. I argued that the history which provides the basis for that reflection is more importantly the history of enacting the social or institutional relation between selves, and that it properly belongs to that reflection. It is concealed, and the act itself thwarted, because the institution of slavery is founded on the contradictory denial of the mediating selfhood it actualizes and on which it depends.

In this section, I want to pursue the third history concealed in, and belonging to, the slave's emerging selfhood. This is the history of experience per se, the history that I have been recounting as the development of experiencing in the two previous chapters. In this history, we find not only the conditions that drive the individual consciousness to respect its experience as the source of the truth of its selfhood, but also the necessity that this selfhood be enacted or worked out institutionally, that is, in relation to other self-conscious selves.

As in the last section, my goal here is to show how the drama of the master and slave prefigures or anticipates another context for thematizing self-consciously, inductively, the scientific notion of experience. The third and ultimately conclusive context developed in the experience of slavery is experience as such, and it is to that I turn now.

Remember that in the analysis of desiring self-consciousness two important claims were made. The first of these was that self-consciousness had to learn to see its experience as the expression of the self-determining totality which is the truth of its selfhood. This claim was the result of a continuing process of development, beginning in sensuous certainty, that had provided experiential evidence that natural consciousness, which operates by disregarding what its experience tells it, had to be overcome. The development that resulted in this claim then was the development of the concept of experience through the experiencing of individual consciousness.

The second claim was that individual consciousness found an advocate for its experience in the presence of an other who was, like itself, self-conscious. The continuing story of experience rested on just what individual consciousness was able to make of that other self-consciousness, and it is the path from the emergence of the other for-itself to the slave's inductive reflection that comprises the history of the concept of experience organizing and determining the slave's experience. I want to recount here those aspects of that history that have a direct bearing on the experience of slavery, keeping in mind that, as the individual learns ultimately and as my argument is aimed at supporting, the whole of the experience of consciousness has "direct bearing" on every determinate form of conscious life it makes possible.

The desiring self-consciousness experiences the other self-consciousness as a threat. Remember that desiring self-consciousness claimed that it was immediately the truth of all otherness, and from such a perspective, the emergence of an other whose bearing indicates that it too posits itself as the source of all being presents a challenge to the first individual's claim about its selfhood.[29]

The only appropriate response for desiring self-consciousness is to behave precisely as it would in any other encounter with an ostensible other: to consume it, which is to say to destroy its integrity as other. Because desiring self-consciousness defines its own selfhood as the truth of all experiencing, it cannot tolerate the presence of any other claim of this kind. Such an approach must be reciprocated by the other to the extent that it also is a desiring self-consciousness, thus what ensues is a mutual struggle for the consumption of the other.

Victory, in this context, is unsatisfying for the same reason that desiring self-consciousness itself is unsatisfying: its need to have its primacy acknowledged by the capitulation of the other is undermined by its destruction of the other. What sets the experience of the death struggle with an other self-consciousness apart, however, is its potential for revealing to the victor the difference between the living struggle and the hollow victory that attends upon the death of the other combatant. Let me explain.

In joining the struggle, the desiring self-consciousness seeks the destruction, the death, of the other. At the same time, in staking its own life, desiring self-consciousness implicitly expresses the truth that has marked it all along: that it takes existence, its own natural or living involvement with others, to be of no consequence.[30] Desiring self-consciousness is the immediate negation of the constituents of its own life, a life that is, as we have seen, denied independence in the process. At the same time, in its denial of its own living, desiring self-consciousness remains "natural," or destructive of otherness and unable to learn from its other and to develop self-consciousness. We can see that, to the extent that desiring self-consciousness really desires a natural, or abstract, negation of the independence of its life, it desires death.[31] It is only by transforming its desire and by overcoming its natural impassivity and learning to respect its other, an other self-consciousness, that the struggling self-consciousness can escape the cycle of frustrated acts of selfhood.

The struggling self-consciousness provides itself the experience that opens up this option in victory. Victory, the death of the other, provides the survivor with a sharpened awareness of the difference between the living struggle and the nearness of victory, in which its claim to selfhood begins to take shape and the morbid absence which comes with death of the other. The struggle itself and the confirmation of selfhood that is anticipated in the feeling of impending triumph are in stark contrast to the hollowness of an other that is again unable to confirm selfhood.

There are two key lessons about selfhood opened up in the victor's experience of the struggle. The first is that in it, and specifically in the moments approaching victory, the struggling self-consciousness gains a proximity to validating its own vision of selfhood that is not available in any other destructive encounter it may have. That is, in the look of fear and capitulation prior to the other's death, it finds what it has already recognized as a self on the verge of recognizing, in return, its own selfhood. The struggling self-consciousness is able to learn then that its own selfhood *is* to the extent that it is actively being recognized by an other experiencing self as the truth of its experience.[32]

The key to realizing this lesson lies, in turn, in another. To learn that it is in fact dependent on the recognition of an other self, the struggling self-consciousness must learn that it is equally dependent on another 'other': life itself. That is, it must learn to recognize the relationship between the living struggle for recognition and the emptiness of validating its authority over an other's dead body. Indeed, to learn how to escape the desire for death that characterizes natural consciousness as a whole, struggling self-consciousness has to assert as its own truth its dependence on life.[33] This it does in seeking living recognition from another, something it can only do as a living being preparing for selfhood by investigating its experience.

This allows us to revise the description of self-consciousness we were left with at the end of the last chapter. Not only must desiring self-consciousness learn to respect life as its own being and to investigate it inductively, but it also must enlist any other self-consciousness to participate. The authority of any selfhood it uncovers in its experience is real only to the extent that other selves recognize it as the truth of their experience. Not only must self-consciousness be inductive then it must in some sense be consensual or communal. The selfhood that reflects the truth of experience is real only to the extent that it is a *universal* self, a self shared by others *qua* experiencing selves and which organizes relations between selves.

To accept the necessity of actively seeking the recognition of an other self then is both to make explicit and to invert the hierarchy adopted in desire. The primacy of pure selfhood assumed by desiring self-consciousness now becomes the mantle worn by the other, whose recognition becomes essential, and the individual self-consciousness is forced to take as its own role the dependent condition of living in preparation for selfhood, a kind of preselfhood, or the condition of mere life.

This deferral of selfhood becomes its definition of, or its claim about, selfhood—that it is something my living prepares me for and that will come to me from a self-constituting self. It is in this respect that Hegel's remark about "consciousness in the form of thinghood"[34] is to be understood: in its indeterminate or predeterminate being, the self-consciousness that emerges from the death struggle is like the potential thing of ordinary conscious life, indeterminately dependent on the field of perceptibility and somehow thrown forward into thinghood by it. The link is that it is an object-to-be, determinate only to the extent that it is awaiting some contingent act of confirmation or realization.

It is important to see here too how the slave and master emerge from, and belong to, the individual consciousness. The individual recognizes (and this becomes central in my next chapter) the necessity for its own claim about selfhood, that it be recognized by an other self, that the other *confer* selfhood. The master is this other, preexistent self that belongs (implicitly) to the slave's self-consciousness, and the slave the inchoate object-to-be that belongs to the master's.

We now can see how the slave's drive to be confirmed by the master within the institution of slavery is a necessary development in the education of self-consciousness and why it provides that education, according to the terms of the living selfhood the slave works out in its labor. The master's threat of death is precisely what the slave needs to learn, thus needs to confirm what was implicit in becoming a slave at all: its escape from natural self-consciousness.

This is why the slave's potential discovery of selfhood depends on experiencing "the absolute Lord," or death. Confronting and accepting its own mortality means the slave has learned the difference between itself and something merely natural, and that lesson is what it makes explicit by renouncing slavery for stoicism in the name of its selfhood. Notice too that in failing to experience a similar threat, the master is doomed to learn the hard way the lesson the threat makes explicit for the slave.

It is life in the face of one's own death that brings the urgency needed to kick start the learning process. Death would confirm that the slave was indeed merely natural, an independence to be negated, and by incorporating it as a constant possibility for itself the slave has already become tacitly conscious of itself and made its existence a possible object of self-consciousness. The persistent nature of the threat and the ability to stave it off in shaping the object of the master's will mean the slave is forced to learn about its living, developing selfhood, something that was only made possible by embracing the deferral of selfhood and the identity with life. The slave's experience then fulfils the project of becoming a self by virtue of living as the object for an other self.

As was the case for the institutional dimension of the slave's experience, the history belonging to the concept of experience stays hidden in the inductive reflection that drives it into stoicism. There is a much sharper distinction, however, between the experience of itself gained through its work and the phenomenological analysis of the conditions leading to slavery than there was between its work and its role as slave for the master.

Simply put, just as the institution of slavery is founded on denying its selfhood while providing the context in which it can be uncovered, the *experience* of slavery only arises to the extent that the individual already lacks the kinds of phenomenological categories necessary for recounting as its own the conceptual history of experience. In fact, the events recounted as that history are the construction of those categories, and only the culminating inductive reflection will have been prepared to tell that story.

Conclusion

What I have done in this chapter is to lay out the preliminary conception of induction that is the focus of the development of self-consciousness in the drama of the master and slave. I showed how the slave's attempts to satisfy the master provided it with an experiential basis for an inductive claim about its selfhood. Specifically, I argued that the slave's need to learn to achieve the results demanded by the master, and its constant fear of death at the hands of the master, forced it to act without knowing exactly what to do and to investigate its experience to learn how to better realize its goal. The slave learns through fear and labor that it is the singular center of experiencing, the mediating agency of universal selfhood.

Specifically, the slave learns that its life is the principle determining the relationship between itself and its experienced other, and that the differences that matter for it are those between the world as securing its survival and the world as it is. In other words, the slave learns from its experience of surviving, inductively, that it is the unity of living selfhood, which is self-differentiating, -mediating, and -comprehending as a self-maintaining center of being.

But we then turned to describe the limits to the slave's discovery. That this inductive selfhood was still in-itself was reflected in the immediacy with which slave and master confront one another and in the concealed mediation of each by the other. To uncover the limits of the slave's inductive act of self-consciousness, I turned to two further dimensions of the slave's experience, which actively determined the experience of slavery and, as such, properly belonged to any complete claim about the truth of that experience. The first of these was the institution of slavery, the principled relationship between the universal selfhood of the master and the singular selfhood of the slave. The second, the developing concept of experiencing, showed both *why* desiring self-consciousness enters institutional experience and *how* that institution has to be developed to fulfil the objectives of the experiencing individual investigating its experience inductively. In both cases, the fuller sense of selfhood was concealed by the inability of the institution of slavery to accommodate the recognition of the role of the master's universality on the part of the slave, the subordination of inductive singularity to universality, and its inability to accommodate the recognition of the universality of active singularity, its place as the self-mediating life of universality.

In the next chapter, we will address the question of the institution itself and trace the development of institutional life as it comes to recognize experiencing singularity as its own self-mediation, a necessary moment in the self-differentiating unity of self-conscious selfhood.

CHAPTER FOUR

The Experience of the Institutional Self

Introduction

In the first chapter, we discussed sensuous certainty, the claim that experiencing simply happens, or is immediate. But immediate experiencing proved impossible, because experiencing showed itself to demand that any determinate content be singled out of an already unified manifold of possible content. Consciousness, we learned, is only possible on the basis of this prior unity.

Everyday consciousness is content to continue to single out perceptible details as representative of real manifold units, or things, without making the relationship between them an explicit concern. I argued that perception, or everyday awareness, is inductive in-itself because it has responded to the experienced necessity of organizing its experience in this way and posited an indeterminate unity as that which both preserves and makes accessible to consciousness the perceptible details of conscious life.

This inconspicuous relationship proves problematic, however, and leaves everydayness prone to error. Because it takes this unity to be both indeterminate and immediately objective, perception has trouble holding details and unities together, and in response to its insecurity we saw two forms of reflective and comprehensive consciousness attempt to meet the challenge of securely organizing the multiplicity of perceptible details in the form of its governing or universal unity. Consciousness, in other words, recognized the need to *know* what was going on in its experience.

In the second chapter, I looked at the two forms knowledge takes in trying to solve the problem of experiencing.

The first of these, the understanding, pursues unity at the expense of the multiplicity of perceptible details. We learned from its experience that the unity that knowing seeks cannot be held at the expense of determinate details. The unity of an experienced manifold entails its own differences, the differences governed by its concept. The unity the understanding posits can only hope to account for differences it is already responsible for, the cognitive gymnastics it is driven to in order to salvage its project. We saw that the activity of experiencing consciousness had taken the form of such a self-differentiating unity. But for the understanding, the recognition that the only differences it is able to reconcile are its own spells the end of its goal of comprehending objectivity as such.

The challenge of comprehending experience, then, was a concern for self-consciousness, which took on all experienced forms of objectivity as aspects of its own activity. Desiring self-consciousness, picking up where the understanding left off, posited itself as the immediate unity of experiencing consciousness, and so failed to respect the differences we had already encountered in the development of experiencing consciousness. The failure of desiring self-consciousness was its inability to see these differences, its own differences, as mediating the unity of its selfhood, or as self-mediating. These differences do not make a difference for desiring selfhood, thus it fails to come to terms with the conditions for its own self-constituting reflection. In its blindness to the specific differences of its own experience, desiring self-consciousness condemns itself to the same natural logic that we have seen belongs to its proper object, conscious life.

Both the understanding and desiring self-consciousness attempt to posit as the truth of experience an a priori unity that was indifferent to experiencing, with the result that each ended up asserting an immediate (and tautologous) identity: it must be it, and I am I, respectively. The key to developing self-consciousness, we learned, lies in its ability to recognize its experience, its own difference, as mediating its identity. We saw that self-consciousness has to identify itself with and to investigate its experiencing and to learn from it *inductively* or *on its own terms* how selfhood functions as its truth.

But the commitments of desiring self-consciousness are only challenged in the experience of an other self-consciousness whose own claim to be the truth of experiencing presents the first self-consciousness with the brute fact of having its immediate authority challenged, or mediated, by its experience. The presence of the other self demands that the first prove its claim, that it win that truth as a concession from the other. Self-conscious selfhood can only be achieved if this and any other selves recognize its authority. The truth of selfhood has to take the form of a universal self, which governs all experiencing selves and which they too recognize inductively as the truth of their experience.

In the first stage of its inductive education, the individual self-consciousness gave up its claim to primacy to an other self in order to survive its challenge and to prepare itself for realizing its universal selfhood. In the institution of slavery, it learns that its own inductive singularity, its own ability to organize and transform the determinations of the natural world on the basis of what it learns from experience, is a necessary moment in the truth of its experiencing selfhood. But its perspective is distorted by the institution it enters in conceding its primacy. The conditions of its concession are such that the master views the slave not as a moment of the master's universal authority, but (like desiring self-consciousness before it) as a mere life of no consequence to selfhood. The master takes its authority to be immediate, thus loses sight of the slave's work in realizing the master's institutional authority by recognizing it in every act. The fear of the master, or the fear of death which haunts the slave as the legacy of the moment of challenge and its ensuing struggle, transforms an institutionally universal form of self-consciousness into a struggle for mere life. The master's presence as threatening the existence of the slave forces the slave to adapt its inductive singularity to the conditions of mere survival. The institution of slavery transforms the act of identifying with a universal self into a confrontation with the productive vitality of singular selfhood. The slave identifies itself explicitly with the act of experiencing as a form of independent conscious life, to the extent that the authority of the master self, and of the institution as a whole, is taken to be an authority that immediately confronts it and thereby appears to be external. Our analysis of the experience of self-consciousness showed us why the combined objectives of relating to other selves and learning from experience initially takes this one-sided form and reveals that slavery is *self-instituted*: it is the result of the work of the singular self responding to its developing comprehension of experience and recognizing its constitutive universality in the act of instituting its self-comprehension.

Having learned that its selfhood must take the form of a social universality, or be instituted in an authoritative relation to other selves, experiencing consciousness can only find the externality of authority alienating, or a barrier to recognizing the self-consciousness already at work in the institution. If it is to complete the project of self-knowledge, it has to develop an institutional life in which it recognizes universal or institutional authority as its own, and in which its inductively mediating singularity is recognized in turn as the self-mediation of universality.[1] In other words, it must, like the slave, learn to work on and transform its objective situation to realize by means of that labor a relationship to its governing authority, one that reflects the experience of institutional life. This transformation, again like the slave's, must be worked out in and as the context of experiencing self-consciousness, which is to say inductively. That toward which the development of institutional systems is driving is precisely the recognition of the constitutive role of the inductive identification made by the member of the society with its governing selfhood. Finally, we will see in this process transformative induction in the institutional context, what we typically call, following Hegel, world history.[2]

In this chapter we will shift our focus to the development of institutional life. My goal here is to describe the movement within the logic of the institution toward the recognition of the singular selves as the self-mediating activity of the universal selfhood. That is, we will be watching the way in which institutions develop to reflect their dependence on the inductive initiative of singular selves in identifying as the truth of their experience the authority of institutionally sanctioned selfhood, or spirit.

This development will occur in three stages. In the first, the institution of *Sittlichkeit* will posit the immediate universality of some of its constituents in the form of a natural authority like the master's and thereby immediately exclude their inductively singular act of identifying that universality as the truth of their experience. The immediate exclusion of the determinate identification by living, experiencing selves leads *Sittlichkeit* into crisis because it is responsible for creating a counter-authority, an institution within *Sittlichkeit* that gathers around the excluded moment of the natural or unwittingly reflective selfhood and celebrates its authority. The crisis of institutional failure takes the form of a reversion into the pre-institutional death struggle, as it reveals that the specific institution has not realized explicitly what it has committed to implicitly in organizing itself institutionally. For *Sittlichkeit*, this means the struggle between its own institutions.

The institution of *Bildung*, which develops from the transitional stage of the institution that recognizes the legal rights of the person, inverts the logic of *Sittlichkeit* and places full authority in the singular act of reflective or inductive identification. Once again, however, it posits an immediate antithesis between natural or determinate selfhood and the transforming singularity that is immediately universal by repudiating determinateness. But because the moment of singularity is irremediably determinate, *Bildung*, like *Sittlichkeit*, is divided against itself, culminating in the war against determinate selves that pits each against the other in the self-destruction of the Terror.

The development culminates in the institution of morality and its determination as conscience. In conscientious selfhood, the necessity of carrying out one's duty forces each self to identify as the universally necessitated selfhood an act of inductive singularity. The authority of universal selfhood recognizes the necessarily determinate or situated nature of singularity, but equally posits its ability to learn from its experience what is universal in it. The institution of conscience prepares us for the final development of inductive selfhood, its realization as inductive in-and-for-itself or as absolute knowing.[3]

The Experience of Sittlichkeit

Self-consciousness must undertake the same laborious transformation of the experienced immediacy of its institutional being that it has already undertaken with respect to the experienced immediacy of its singular being. As a result, the stages in developing an adequate institutional basis for the articulation of selfhood will reflect the struggle against immediacy we have already encountered in the analysis of natural consciousness. This is perhaps clearest in *Sittlichkeit*, which is founded on the immediate or natural necessity that conscious life be instituted. What it will demonstrate, therefore, is the need for institutional life to learn to recognize the self-determining mediation, or singularity, of its members.

The institution of *Sittlichkeit*, presented as the world of the ancient Greek city state and its transition into the Roman Empire, is characterized by the tension between its being-for-self, its *mediated* realization through the concrete acts in which its members freely identify themselves with it as their substance and the way it expresses its own authority to itself as *immediate*. *Sittlichkeit* is the institution that understands its being-for-self in terms of the natural logic of a universal or institutional self that is immediately the truth of the individuals who are its members, but whose authority is realized through the mediation of merely determinate or natural community. Like the self-consciousness of desire, *Sittlichkeit* experiences itself consciously, that is, as the need to overcome the "objective" distinction between apparently natural or particular individuals and those individuals as self-conscious citizens of the community. While it tacitly recognizes the appearance of individuals who are *really* citizens as a necessary moment in their true reflection into citizens, it denies the act in which they themselves would perform such a reflection; it denies, that is, their selfhood as singular selves actively realizing the authority of the state.[4] To be a citizen is to be what one has already been, without ever having explicitly chosen this identity.[5] The dialectic of *Sittlichkeit* traces the crisis implicit in its tacit dependence on being recognized by its members as their truth and the divisions that have arisen within it as a result of the suppression of this dependence in the form of an immediate or natural authority. That is, in positing its authority as immediate, it has precluded recognition of the mediation of particularity enacted under its authority, thus the moment of particularity will always take the form of an apparent outside.[6]

The life of *Sittlichkeit* reflects the tension between its natural authority and its self-consciously mediated life under that authority in the division of the moment of singularity into the apparently natural (or particular) individuals and real (universal) citizens. Since citizenship is a *naturally* self-conscious reflection on the community of selves, it must acknowledge the authority of the logic of the natural order, and so it has its counterpart in the merely natural community. Because the members as living are equally immediately or naturally tied to one another as family, the family emerges as an institution in its own right, over and against the state. The very existence of natural authority in the state necessarily reproduces itself in the natural authority of the family, thus the universal institution gives rise to a particular one within itself.[7]

Because each exists in and as an instituted or developed self-conscious totality, each emphasizes the way its members are recognized *as* members. The immediacy of membership and the repudiation of singular action that define each institution mean that membership is defined by obedience to law as custom and as duty. While each is supported by its appropriate law, the two institutions reflect the immediacy of membership in the unquestioned loyalty the member pays to custom and duty.[8]

The family unit governs itself according to the divine law,[9] which immediately assigns identities to its members.[10] In living out these roles, each is recognized solely in terms of the natural or blood relations that bind them. That this community is itself an act of the self-consciousness of the excluded moment of particularity means that it must find some way to recognize the particular individual in its truth. Because the nation claims to be the reality of its citizens and denies that their lives could in any way mediate that reality, and because the family is equally committed (as we will see below) to denying *both* the ethical life of the member (it belongs to the self-as-citizen) *and* the family life of the member (because the family, too, is immediately defined), the individual is recognized only in death, in the funeral ritual.[11]

In the funeral ceremony, the family celebrates its departed member as something 'more than just a life,' but equally as something 'more than just a citizen.'[12] The role of the family member is ultimately defined only negatively because all that is left to the individual is the exclusion of the specific modifications of its identity undertaken in developing itself, its family, and its citizenship,[13] as "accidents,"[14] the exclusion of its citizenship, and *(qua* self-consciousness) the exclusion of its natural life—in other words, what is excluded from the identity of the family member in the ritual of burial is anything that would mark him/her as a finite, singular self responding to its experience as such.[15]

For the nation, citizenship is equally defined by a relationship to death, although in the context of the self-consciously active or actualizing life of the community, this means one's readiness to stake one's life in war.[16] The various social, familial, and economic initiatives which occur in and as the life of the community are merely tolerated, unconsciously recognized, and in the call to arms, dissolved. For the nation, membership equals readiness to fight to the death, and in its call to war it expresses the paradigmatic claim of the nation on its citizens. The warring citizen has recognized the highest duty of civic life, because in joining the fight it has denied that significance of its natural individuality and identified itself with the absolute claim over its being: the nation.[17] The life between wars is nothing, claims the nation, and the ceremonial military parade provides the nation's counterpart to the family's funeral.

In the context of inductive self-consciousness, two issues must be addressed. I have already noted that in denying the significance of the reflective act of identifying the civic or family self as a moment in the life of self-conscious institutions, the realms or "forces"[18] ensure that membership is achieved only consciously, in terms of the immediate authority of the community as a whole. There is no room in the institutions of *Sittlichkeit* for each and every individual self-consciously recognizing the authority of the two realms in an inductive reflection on experience, or as something experience has taught them. Of course, that is exactly why *Sittlichkeit* is a form of natural consciousness: it assigns one-sided significance to the immediate totality of selfhood (the family, the nation) to the exclusion of its actively self-mediating members.[19] The members are literally "understood" to be identified with the larger whole. For both institutions, the decision to recognize oneself as a family member or as a citizen could only trivialize what has already been the necessary legitimizing context to its existence. Neither institution allows the individual to freely identify with that necessity on its own, thus each achieves self-consciousness as a whole by denying it in part. For the singular individual, the experience of selfhood involves "remembering" that it always has been constrained in the service of a transcendent self.[20]

But the life of both institutions *is* something that determines and shapes its members. We have seen how the fulfillment of duty or familial custom is, in every case, a realization of the authority of those institutions that can only occur if singular selves understand or recognize themselves to be commanded by that authority, and act accordingly. The paradigmatic expression of the necessity of singular acts of recognition is not acting in line with this or that duty or custom but in recognizing one set of laws over another. However much the two institutions and their respective laws are predicated on immediate acts of identification, acts which aren't really changing anything at all, each tacitly recognizes that its members' lives are mediated by (excluding) the other.[21]

Here, the contradictory denial of and dependence on the act of the singular self becomes a self-destructive force. In both cases, membership in one institution is at the very least a product of denying membership in another. Members must learn from their experience of the life of both institutions where they must find the truth of that experience. While the man provides material support for the family and is the reason the existence of the family is tolerated at all,[22] he is actualized in the community as a citizen by denying the truth of his family life. Similarly, the woman who devotes herself to what is essentially a life of labor for the nation that tolerates the laws and customs of the family with which she is identified must deny the ultimacy or the truth of the nation.

This sets the stage for the crisis that belongs to the experience of *Sittlichkeit*. To the extent that a member of either institution, in response to conflicting demands, publicly acts on the basis of an exclusive identification with one law, she or he has exposed *Sittlichkeit*'s contradictory demands on the singular self in terms of the hidden structural organization of the community as a whole, or she or he has exposed how the exclusion of the life of the singular self is contradicted by the exclusivity of one set of laws. The act of decision reveals, in other words, the exclusionary and contradictory demands on which the institution is founded, by cutting loose from one community in an act of identifying with the other. The self, in having to decide to which institution she or he belongs, reveals an underworld of mediating influences set in motion by *Sittlichkeit*'s very claim to immediacy.

In terms of the inductive recognition of the truth of selfhood, the act in which the member identifies itself with the institution it takes to represent the truth of its experience, the individual is driven to identify with one institution by denying the truth of its experience of the other. It is forced to reject its involvement in the institution which has shaped it, by rejecting the principle which has informed its experience.

From the standpoint of the institution of *Sittlichkeit*, it is forced to confront the way in which membership depends on the act of singular choice, on the inductive reflection it has refused to acknowledge in positing its truth as immediate or natural. Like the natural forms of consciousness we have already examined, however, it refuses to accept the role of choice and finds itself instead involved in the fateful struggle between divine and human authority.

What begins then as the individual's crime against the set of laws she or he rejects becomes the crime of the individual against her or his *own* laws,[23] and ultimately the crime committed by the very existence of each set of laws against the other:[24] demanding that the individual actively deny the truth of the experience that belongs to it as the condition for its self-consciousness.

To the extent that this outcome is, as Hegel calls it, the "dreadful fate"[25] of *Sittlichkeit*, my analysis has pointed to the logic of natural consciousness as its source. The denial of the mediating agency of singular selves, in the name of an immediate self-identity, *must* frustrate institutional self-consciousness because the living work of singularity is what it depends on for its realization. The crisis brought on by *Sittlichkeit* expresses the same contradiction that confronted desiring or natural self-consciousness as the dilemma of surrendering its supposed immediacy and learning to recognize its own determinacy as built upon the work it undertook in its name, or of continuing the endless frustration of claiming to be the truth of something that, for it, has no intrinsic significance.

Just as the immediacy of desire prevented it from recognizing the living totality that was its proper object, so too do the family and nation turn against the members who provide them with their living actuality. The truth of *Sittlichkeit* necessarily includes the work of singular individuals in recognizing that truth, sacrificing their own claims to primacy in its name. The crisis that arises within or between its institutions lies in its refusal to reciprocate the sacrifice and in the divisions that emerge as a result of its appeal to immediacy.

The singular selfhood which actualizes the institutions of *Sittlichkeit* can only find itself reflected, like the slave, outside the institution which denies it. But because we are now examining those forms of conscious life which self-consciously identify themselves with institutions, singular selfhood emerges in the institution which inverts the one-sided sacrifice of *Sittlichkeit*: the institution of the legal status of the person. Because this is in many ways a transitional stage into the world of *Bildung*, I will follow Hegel in analyzing it briefly.

First, it is important to see that the transition from *Sittlichkeit* to a more responsive form of institutional life is effected as a result of the experience of the inadequacy of the framing logic it enforces. In other words, while *Sittlichkeit* is always ready to explode in kind of self-defeating crisis because of the difficulties concealed in its dualistic communities, that crisis must take the form of some explicit experience of having broken down in its attempt to regulate ways of life. Change occurs in the institutional logic of communities not because someone senses trouble, or analyzes it in advance, but because crisis is endured and responded to. It is in this context that what I am calling induction takes the form of world-history: as Hegel will argue, specific world-historical individuals make these institutional faultlines explicit at some time in a culture's life. Notice, again, that what the institutional context does is to preserve a kind of order in the face of change. It is the stable context that allows and undergoes transformation, providing (as Hegel will argue) the proper object for historical analysis. The logic for historical development, as we will see, will be the need, created by institutional life and experienced by its members, that the experience of individuals be adequately reflected by the legislative practices of the institution.

The institution of legal status is little more than a formal arrangement, a loose frame for freeing up the decision-making work of singular selves. It is identified as a society by the freedom it gives every individual to determine independently the terms of membership. This is a society whose life is comprised of innumerable selves all working in isolation at self-fulfillment in a way that makes any notion of social organization a form of trespass against the rights of the person.

By inverting the emphasis *Sittlichkeit* placed on the community at the expense of the singular self, the world of legal status has made the notion of a shared identity in community impracticable. What defines this institution is precisely the independent, singular nature of the individuals who inhabit it. Any move toward a restriction of their rights as individuals must be seen as an attempt to impose on many some vested interest of another singular member. Indeed, the society of legal status is ruled by just such vested interest, in the form of the aggressive singularity of the emperor.

The absence of a sense of community is crucial to the world of legal status, because again the experience of singularity is devalued. Here, unlike *Sittlichkeit*, it is recognized as that by means of which the laws become real. But that recognition in its one-sided form strips singularity of the possibility of finding the truth of its experience in the selfhood which binds it to others. It is bound to others in asserting its own idiosyncrasies, which is to say it is bound to others in being set apart from them. This is an institution which weakens singularity while exalting it; the institution deprives its members of recognizing the shared organizing principle their singularity is already embracing (implicitly, in the form of the primacy of the singular will) as their truth.

This is the basis for the transition into the world of *Bildung*: the immediate assertion of community and the immediate assertion of singularity have each resulted in an institution at odds with itself over the nature of singularity and over the relationship between the laws of its own determining and the principle of legal recognition as such. The existence of singularity and the difference between the two forms of legal authority are now explicit features of the institution's self-determination, but they are not reconciled. In the world of *Bildung*, we follow the experience of singular selves who have experienced the dissatisfaction of incarnate forms of universally recognized authority and who express their alienation from those established forms by seeking it beyond their limits.[26]

The Experience of Bildung

Hegel's analysis of *Bildung* is a complex phenomenological account of a series of interrelated forms of social alienation, and it is not my intention to reflect all of the intricacies of his account here.[27] Rather, I will show how the institutions of *Bildung* contribute to the development of institutional self-consciousness by further sharpening the tensions between the moments of singularity, particularity, and universality that are at stake in the institutional experience of selfhood.

Specifically, my concern with *Bildung* lies in the way in which each of its institutions attempts to found itself on the ideal of recognizing the actually transformative singularity that the institution of legal selfhood rendered abstractly as a principle. The key here, as it was in the analysis of *Sittlichkeit,* will be to see how the primacy assigned certain logical moments to the exclusion of another works out the necessity of including the omitted term. Like the slave struggling to meet the demands of the master, the institutions of *Bildung* provide us with necessary stages in self-consciously inductive institution-building that culminate in inductive self-consciousness.

Indeed, given that what I am calling the inductive development of the concept of experience is what Hegel calls, in the preface, the *Bildung* of the singular self to the standpoint of science, the institutions collectively called *Bildung* are not surprisingly devoted to instituting the transformative singularity of experiencing. Each is premised on the need for the singular transformation of the determinateness of situated particularity to the universality of selfhood. In recognizing the need for reflective transformation, however, each of these institutions again denies a crucial element of induction: here, the determinateness of the actual situation of developing consciousness.

As a result, the institutions of *Bildung* are epitomized in the need for perpetual revolution. That is, while each demands the repeated reflection on (the poverty of particular) experience, each is committed to denying that any act of transformation could be complete, because as long as the self remains in a particular situation, the need for reflection remains. Before looking in some detail at its resolution in the actual cognition of individual members of *Bildung,* let me describe the logical relations within and between its institutions.

The collapse of the world of *Sittlichkeit* demonstrated the contradictory character of the exclusion of the moment of singularity. The world of the legal self showed how that singularity could not function as an end in itself for a social institution. Both created the difference between the divine law or the *immediate being* of legal authority in-itself and the self-consciously articulated human law by failing to grasp the workings of a self-mediating and self-differentiating totality and left singular selfhood at odds with existing institutions.

In the analysis of *Bildung*, one of Hegel's primary objectives is to show how institutions founded on either the reflected essence of the divine law or the human law, membership in God's family or the rational family of humanity, continually run up against the need for institutions to take concrete, which is to say here, particular, form. Before turning to the two institutions within *Bildung*, let me describe their shared logic in further detail.

The institutions of *Bildung* share a common principle: that the merely natural or actual[28] determinateness of the individual is to be realized in its truth only by identifying it as a product or negation of the universal self.[29] In this respect, these institutions have identified what are for the members of *Sittlichkeit* two opposing realms: the natural and the self-consciously instituted. In the world of *Bildung*, both of the opposed realms of *Sittlichkeit* share a blindness to their instituted state, to their having been produced by self-consciously singular agency.[30]

As I have argued in my analysis of *Sittlichkeit*, it is precisely the barriers created by the assumption of immediate or natural authority on the part of the self-legislated community that tears that world apart. There is then this element to *Bildung* that marks its advance over *Sittlichkeit*. The recognition that both these institutions are the work of developing selves in response to their determinate stations and that they have concealed their involvement in mute reverence for duty and custom belongs to the critical posture of the institutions of *Bildung*. It proposes instead to liberate developing selves from any trappings of immediate or natural authority by identifying its members as purely rational social agents, builders in the great work of creating a life governed only by the freedom of faithful or reasoning self-consciousness.[31]

Membership in this constantly transforming community is defined then by breaking the bonds of determinate authority and by casting off the chains of an inflexible and inherited set of rules and duties. The only real duty here is to make a better life than the one that has been prescribed.[32] The very energy with which each member identifies itself, the powers of faith and reasoning, ensures that this work cannot ever be done "once and for all," but is rather an endless process of building, developing, or bettering what is.

The two most prominent features of the experience of *Bildung* are its negative or destructive attack on determinate forms of selfhood and the limitlessness of its objective. The self committed to *Bildung* espouses a contempt for what is here and now; one is reminded, in Hegel's analysis, of the spirit behind the imperialist conquests of the Americas and Africa and the slaughter of native peoples in the name of progressive civilization. But its contempt knows no bounds—wherever one turns, there are more signs of the energy of reasoning resolved into some form of determinacy and selves prepared to bow before some fetishized authority.

But the limitlessness of its objective ultimately directs it inward, and the self-destruction of *Bildung* in the world of the revolution and terror is its own necessary outcome. My analysis of the institution of slavery suggests why self-destruction follows from the contempt for determinacy: the moment of particularity or determinateness is a necessary one in the life of selfhood. Remember that the slave was able to discover its own singularity as its living productive center, its mediation of its situation. This mediation not only found itself related to determinateness, but it reclaimed determinateness through its singularity as its own—its own results of its labor. What necessitated institutional development was the need to have the experience of this singularity recognized by the institution and the experience of the institution by the singular self. Any institution that demands of the singular self that it repudiate determinateness is ultimately asking it to repudiate singularity, which, when actualized, is precisely what the terror is—the attempt to do away with any expressions of merely particular or determinate singular selves. No objective could ever cease to belong to *this* singular self, or *that* one, and so the project of *Bildung*, which begins by challenging the institutions that depend on its selves, ends by cancelling the selves it depends on.[33]

Like the world of *Sittlichkeit*, the world of *Bildung* is divided into the distinct institutions of faith (or divine law) and enlightenment (or human law), each of which is distinguished from the other by the content of the universal self and by the relationship between that self and the actual situation in which the singular members find themselves.

In the institution of faith, faithful transformation is the only adequate response to the poverty of natural existence. In fleeing the senseless and brutal struggle of the world of legal status, the institution of faith redefines singular selfhood as the basis for reaching beyond and away from that struggle into the pure selfhood of God. Faith involves the renunciation of the natural self of this world in the name of the self that lies beyond apparent actuality. Pure selfhood is for the singular self the higher actuality that awaits it, union with God in God's kingdom, which it prepares itself for by demonstrating its independence from the here and now.[34]

The essential feature of faith is not its exclusion of the natural self, which it shares with the enlightenment, but its exclusion of its pure self from the natural world. For faith, God is something other, something which as a pure self I can identify myself with only conditionally. In making God's will my own, I am in essence identifying with some other than where and when I am, a pure self I can only ever work on behalf of in fleeing the here and now.[35]

The institution of enlightenment opposes itself to faith in denying the need for an 'outside' or beyond in which to realize the identification with universal selfhood. For enlightenment, universal selfhood is the rational self, which each and every self already is. The opposition between faith and enlightenment is not like the tension between the two institutions of *Sittlichkeit*. Rather, the enlightenment is the logical extension of faith, for which faith stands both as an incomplete form of itself and worse, as a threat to its own project of realizing pure selfhood untainted by determinateness. Faith is the "natural" enemy of the enlightenment, because of its desire to demonstrate that faith is really just incompletely self-conscious reason and on its conviction that its impurity poses a threat to realizing a rational community here and now.[36] The project of enlightenment culture is dependent on this critical relation, on presenting itself as the *purer* form of self-consciousness. It is the relativity inherent in enlightenment culture that is its undoing.

The negative attitude adopted by the enlightenment toward faith is equally the struggle between selfhood and the necessity that it have content, or thoughts. The institution of faith, in representing to itself the universal self as the determinate beyond God's kingdom, relies on determinate *thoughts* of selfhood, without recognizing (according to the enlightenment criticism) that all thoughts are the immediate other to selfhood as the power of reasoning, or the singular self transforming its determinateness according to the universal power of selfhood.[37]

What is lost to enlightenment reasoning is the extent to which thoughts belong to reasoning selfhood as its own determinations. Just as we saw with slavery, the products of singularity are that with which it begins and that into which it is resolved; singularity is framed by determinateness. The primacy the enlightenment assigns to the activity of reasoning selfhood cannot be maintained without thoughts, and the practice of critical insight necessarily depends on the very determinateness it negates. Its negativity is both what feeds on, and thereby blinds it to, the significance of its situation. As we will see, without the workings of faith as its object, the enlightenment is reduced to the pure energy of reasoning, which is a self-consciously instituted vision of the supersensible beyond of the understanding and its opposing moment of determinate singularity. To have any content at all, it must be mediated by the determinate features noticed by experiencing consciousness.[38]

Resemblances to the understanding aside, the more apt comparison is to desiring self-consciousness. As a form of self-consciousness, desire overlooked the determinate situation it encountered to dissolve any determinate shapes of experiencing consciousness in the abstract and immediate unity of self-consciousness. For desire, all determinate consciousness was a one-sided abstraction from the true unity of the self, moments lacking reality and for the immediate consumption of desire, simply vanishing challenges to its authority.[39] The behavior, such as it was, of desiring self-consciousness, consisted in an open-ended attack on all forms of consciousness, that is, all ways of maintaining that the truth of experience was some form of objective being. Because of its impassivity with respect to acts of experiencing, desire was unable to learn what it was and was left with the "empty tautology" of an abstract self-identity as its claim about the truth of experience.[40]

The behavioral characteristics of the individual members of enlightenment culture differs from desire in three important respects. First, self-consciousness has now been determined as reason, or as the reasoning activity of singular selves. It is a determinately reflective relationship that knows the difference between the particular instances of selfhood and their reflection into the essence of selfhood as reasoning. Second, enlightenment consciousness is institutional: it recognizes its community with other reasoning selves as a necessary moment in its truth, whereas desiring self-consciousness took up only its own determinate moments of consciousness, of its own singularity, and only then to pronounce them mere appearances. For the enlightenment consciousness, the truth of reasoning is the truth belonging to all selves.

Finally, for desiring self-consciousness, the objective world of perception and the understanding was abandoned as a property of the illusory object-orientation of consciousness. The world of things was just a feature of its appearance as independent. For enlightenment consciousness, however, individual selves and their determinate thoughts *separately* take on the immediate significance attributed to experience by sensuous certainty.[41] Let me pursue this parallel further to draw out of it the seeds of the crisis that befalls enlightenment culture.

Despite their differences, enlightenment consciousness is committed to the same project of dissolving particular acts of experiencing which defines desire, and paradoxically the differences I have described serve to sharpen both its hostility to experiencing selfhood and the crisis of the enlightenment—from death struggle to social self-destruction.

In its relationship to faith, enlightenment culture is critical of the impurity of self-consciousness that holds fast to any determinate thought. In contrast to the way in which faith presents its own thoughts to itself as the pure being of selfhood, or God, the enlightenment identifies with a vacuous absolute—its only content is the behavior of faith, whose determinations it strips from faith as superstition. Pure reasoning self-consciousness knows itself to be other than, or the enemy of, any thought. It is the active generation and manipulation of thought. Any determinate description of its pure being could only be made from the standpoint of faith.[42]

In its critical activity, enlightenment reasoning strips from the self-conscious energy of faith not only faith's thoughts, or its properties, but its objects, the mere things it employs as standard bearers for its absolute. In its attack on faith, while it rightly identifies thoughts as the work of faithful self-consciousness, it wrongly attributes to faith a fetish for mere things. That is, it excludes from the thought the being of its object—a move which seems regressive in the context of a more developed self-consciousness than we encountered in desire.[43]

What we can see in enlightenment reasoning then is the way in which the act of criticism expresses its reliance on the particular singularity of consciousness as a necessary moment in its critical truth. That is, for the self-consciousness which *is* by attacking the determinate shape self-consciousness attaches to itself, there corresponds the need for a positive selfhood in the form of an abstractly singular being responding to its immediately indeterminate other. While determinate singularity is recognized within reasoning only as a negative moment, it is a moment posited by enlightenment reasoning as that of which it is the truth, as the object reasoning needs for its transformation into selfhood. The enlightenment has to recognize situated singularity to dissolve its determinateness. As

Hegel notes, it is an absolute truth of enlightenment reasoning, a moment differentiated by and mediating for the enlightenment project.[44]

This is why enlightenment reasoning arrives at sensuous certainty.[45] In its need for determinate expressions of singularity, it turns on all of the shapes of experiencing consciousness we have observed so far and negates each of them as it does faith. Like the sacred object that is reduced to a product of the fetishes of faith and distinguished from mere being, the experienced world of consciousness is reduced to the pure being that sensuous certainty claimed for its object. It is precisely because it is a *more* developed form of self-consciousness than desire that it is able to distinguish situated experiencing singularity as the "natural" or undeveloped moment in selfhood and to direct itself against this moment in all of its forms. Enlightenment reasoning is the attack on all developed expressions of experiencing singularity, but it cannot dispense with that moment of situated singularity.

The critical energy of enlightenment culture, as we have seen, isn't bound by its engagement of faith. Nor is it bound by the epistemological types we have encountered; it is the necessary extension of its project to take on all determinate social institutions. That is, it must ultimately direct its energies at the embodied or determinate institutions it finds around it, and no longer externally, or critically, but on their own terms—actually tearing down the fixed social order. In this way, its relationship to the thought of determinate singularity becomes an actual revolution.

It is a revolution that can end only in death, because it has as its natural enemy the natural or determinate self; and, like desire, it is the death of slaughter, the death in which no one death could satisfy it, because in its singularity it would still offend. As we have already seen, this is a part of the truth of selfhood, a truth that even the enlightenment has recognized. The death it is committed to as the truth of any determinate form must be brought down on its own members, their irremediable determinacy, and on itself as an institution of revolution—indeed, its final form is the deeply conservative terror. Precisely what the experience of *Bildung* shows us is that the isolation of singularity is an ineradicable, or universal, aspect of self-consciousness.[46] The revolution and the Terror (in which the guillotine serves to reinforce the immediacy with which determinate singularity is excluded from culture) fulfil the natural logic of *Bildung*, in which the necessary moment of self-mediating selfhood is immediately excluded from its universal truth only in self-annihilation.

The crisis of the Terror then realizes the contradiction of an immediately universal self and poses for experience the necessity of reconciling the moments of determinate singularity and universality. This reconciliation takes us to the institution of morality.

Morality and Conscience

In the last section, the drive to reform institutional life drew experiencing consciousness away from the merely natural form of ethical life into a commitment to a reforming culture, which as an institution was organized around a universal selfhood that denied the influence of any particular determination on its capacity to realize itself as universal. In morality, we have that institution which recognizes the moment of situated singularity as a formal or conceptual distinction in the universal will. It is the institution founded on the project of *overcoming* one's situation by identifying with the universal will. That is, it is the institution which recognizes the unity of the moments of selfhood we have experienced—determinate singularity and universality—as its objective. Within the institution of morality, we will find the same kind of development that we have seen in the other institutions, in which a founding principle is mediated by the experience it makes possible.

The moral world in which we begin this experience is then the world made right by rational reflection. That is, singular selves recognize the call of duty and recognize it as the call to adopt the standpoint of the universal will. In the realization of duty, however, morality in turn recalls the basic tension within *Bildung*. Action in response to duty necessarily depends on the situation the moral self finds itself in, both with respect to knowing or recognizing duty as it arises, in knowing how to act, and in being able to carry out its duty. But the world of singular selves remains a *natural* world, that is, a world that hasn't developed according to the universal will, and cannot. In this sense, the world of morality speaks of an incomplete reconciliation of the two forms of selfhood described in *Sittlichkeit*: I must know when to choose the universal selfhood (of the male citizen) from out of my natural day-to-day experiencing. The incompleteness comes from the opposition between the two, the need to choose one to the exclusion of the other, and in the primacy of the moral domain for realizing what it means to be a self.

The institution of morality begins then with the same tension that has plagued all the previous forms of institutional consciousness and consciousness in general between a posited immediate or natural distinction and an activity whose intrinsic mediation has to challenge or threaten that immediacy. In this case, morality is divided between the immediately natural world of the singular self and the reality that world has for the self as a universal self. Because every act of duty must bridge this divide and so contaminate moral universality, the moral act itself is a subversion of the principle of duty. Let me examine this problem.

Morality, like the understanding, operates according to a fundamental dualism: there is a world of natural or experienced disorder that the understanding converts to unity, stability, and permanence—to truth, according to the understanding. In a similar manner, morality assigns to self-consciousness the reality of all that is. Once reflectively captured in the moral knowledge we can have of the world, what is becomes what is as it ought to be. The task, as Hegel describes it, is to transform mere nature, devoid of moral worth and the selfhood that recognizes duty, into something consistent with the moral knowledge selfhood has.

But this means that morality, like the understanding, must bring together the sensuous reality that it experiences as nature and the pure rational selfhood it knows as conforming to duty. In other words, morality like the understanding must admit the mediation of what it claims is pure by that which it has defined its purity in opposition to. Morality and the understanding take the forms of projects that are posited as in some sense having already been completed under terms that threaten the possibility of such completion. There must be only the pure truth of morally reflected or understood reality, and yet to get it means having to transform an experienced reality that it cannot incorporate and remain itself.

The expression of the impossibility emerges in the experience of morality in a manner that clearly recalls the experience of the understanding. If, as a moral self, I must make things right and in accordance with the duty described by a pure will, then my initial encounter with nature and natural (dis)order will present what gets called an "interface" problem: how can a pure will describe duty in terms that enable me to make sense of the complexity of a nature that is impure, disorganized, and so on? As was the case in the experience of the understanding, the hostility to a natural world which might mediate the truth attained by morality is doubly crippling: not only can it not admit the need to adapt its duties to meet the specific demands of the world in which it must act, but the outcome of moral action—the organization of nature by means of adapted duties—would amount to confirming the insufficiency of moral selfhood and its pure actuality. Moral self-consciousness, however, is faced with the alternative of acting on these crippling and contradictory demands, or admitting that the moral world is unreal, and merely an ideal.

Conscience emerges as the response to this unbridgeable divide, in the form of the self that knows it must act to carry out its duty, no matter what. The conscientious self is the self that places the need to realize its duty above the complications that morality produces. Unlike the reflective act of moral abstraction, conscience posits the necessity of action under the conditions of a limited or situated singularity as the universally recognized truth of experiencing, not in conceptual terms, but in its acting.

In this respect, conscience is first of all an ethical reflex, not a scientific standpoint. In our analysis of the experience of conscience, we will find that it has *implicitly* realized the unified concept of experiencing selfhood, the concept of a *self-differentiating, self-mediating, and self-comprehending experience*, but that this concept is for conscience initially concealed or only what it is in-itself. Conscientious selfhood is the institutionally self-conscious form of perceiving consciousness, the inductive response to experiencing that posits not the unity of the thing as the medium of properties but the inductive response to social self-consciousness that posits its own determinate singularity as the thing that actively includes some duties and excludes others. With conscience then we have the lived truth of everyday experiencing, in the form of the singular self that knows that it is responsible for the necessity of singling this out and not that.[47]

In conscience, the activity of the singular self is knowing transformed into necessitated action. Conscience claims to know the truth of the world in the act of making it right. Its cognitive ambitions now have been identified as the power of being convinced that what it does counts as its universal objective.

But conscience as a knower isn't simply positive. In its responsibility to its situation and its ability to find within that situation the form of action appropriate to a self acting out of duty, conscience is *inductive*. The singular self, in acting conscientiously, recognizes that it must act universally according to the limits of its station and takes upon itself the task of uncovering the universality expressed in its situation, its experience. Conscientious selfhood demands that the self live up to the demands of universality, even in its concrete and limited perspective. It hasn't abolished the ideal of morality but actualized it, brought it down to earth.

The conscientious self, therefore, has to undertake a thorough examination of its experience to find the unified expression of universally necessitated selfhood. It has, implicitly at least, fulfilled the first challenge facing desiring self-consciousness: it knows its true self only upon inductively gathering it from the disparate features of its situation, its experience.[48]

It has equally met the challenge of consensual induction, however, which has been the challenge animating the history of institutional life I have been describing in this chapter. It is a defining feature of conscience as institutional that in its acting it has identified the singular self as the universal self, that is, that it transforms its living singularity in accordance with the necessity expressed in its experienced institutional totality.[49] In acting, conscience publicizes its identification with the universal and implicitly offers it to the conscientious community to be recognized as universal. By actualizing its universality in action, the conscientious self has broken the abstract isolation of moral selfhood with a *social expression of the universality of singular selfhood.*[50] The very necessity it enacts, its *conviction*, is its knowledge that, despite its determinateness, it acts in a way that others will recognize.[51]

At the same time, in exposing itself to consensual confirmation, the conscientious self implicitly acknowledges an antithesis between concretely situated action and the universal self it has identified with in acting. It knows it lacks the perspective of other situated selves, and worse, that the comprehensive survey of its experience which the mantel of universality entails is beyond its scope—precisely because it cannot include, but must recognize, its difference from other singular selves.[52] Conscientious selfhood is as singular as it is universal, and its singularity confronts

> a plurality of circumstances which breaks up and spreads out endlessly in all directions, backwards into their conditions, sideways into their connections, forward in their consequences.[53]

While it is convinced of its own sufficiency, the conscientious self recognizes a gap: the immediate difference between its singular self 'making things right' as best it can and the scope of the circumstances it confronts and the reverberations it sets off in order to act universally in its duty.

But this difference or antithesis is exactly what we have come to expect from experiencing consciousness which is inductive but not yet for-itself. In taking its circumstances as the expression of a necessitated, universal, conscientious agency, conscience remains committed to the antithesis of universally complex circumstances and singularly articulated necessity because it is the unity of the two that it posits in developing from the crisis of abstraction in moral conscience. As inductive in-itself, conscience does not involve making explicit, or knowing or deriving the totality of its circumstances as the self-differentiated, self-mediated determinations of its universality.[54] It acts upon its ability to organize and recognize a unified and necessary act in response to its concrete situation. In this sense, it *is* this totality of circumstances as *self-comprehending*, but in its own conviction that its act is the right one. In conviction, the unity of the self-comprehension of experienced differences remains veiled, and universality attaches to the act of conscience only as the necessity that it be recognized. It has reached the form of inductively unifying that recognizes its experience as expressive of its universal principle and recognizes experiencing singularity as the means to realize the identity with universality, but this is what we can see in its experience. For conscience, there is only the need to act.

To complete its inductive development, one that began in sensuous certainty, the conscientious self has to experience the gap between its determinate circumstances and its universality and experience the need to unify them.

This experience arises in the need, posited implicitly in the conviction that all other singular selves will respect the necessity that I respond to my situation in just this way, that the self that acts on conviction forgives the selves who do the same.[55] It is in this act of reconciling thought and action, universality and singularity, all of which stand apart for conviction, that the inductive development of the experience of instituted consciousness reaches its final station.

In acting conscientiously, the singular self expresses its knowledge of duty in its act. But there is nothing in the act itself to define it as conscientious, and the guilt experienced in acting out of limited knowledge compromised by its own interests leads the self to be suspicious of others. There has to be some way of distinguishing such acts from merely self-interested ones. That is, just as the self views its own situation to determine what it necessitates *qua* universal self, the self should to be able to view the situation of another to make the same kind of evaluation.

But the criterion of conviction is simply conviction, thus any act, every act, is potentially conscientious. Moreover, the criterion of conviction means that any one self cannot enter into and make distinctions within the singularity of an other. As a member of the community, it has to recognize that other self as genuine, as authentically motivated by what it took to be required by the situation.

This recognition, the forgiveness of the self who acts from conviction, involves actually reconciling the two moments of singularity and universality that were posited as unified by the act of conviction. It is only when the universal forgives, or recognizes as its own, the singular act, that the reciprocal recognition for which institutional life has been striving is realized. To do this again requires an inductive strategy, as the singular forgiving self has to investigate the forms of expressed conviction to learn the universality that comprehends and sanctions it. The universality that recognizes all the forms of singularity, however, is the concept of experience. The reconciliation of the moments specified by forgiveness will be the *knowledge*, as the universal of its singular expressions and as the singular of its identity with the universal in reconciling its singular expressions. The realization of conscience in forgiveness is *phenomenology*, and that leads us to the argument in the next chapter.

Conclusion

We have followed the development of institutional logic to its culmination in the institution which recognizes the authority of singular selfhood to act as universal and demands of the singular self that it identify itself with the universal *inductively*.

To get to this point, we looked at two other institutions, each of which one-sidedly stressed the immediate exclusivity of one moment of the institutional totality: in *Sittlichkeit*, we saw how the exclusion of self-mediation led to the conflict between different institutions that each identified as their truth one of the immediately opposed aspects of selfhood; in the institution of *Bildung*, we watched the exclusion of self-differentiation as the singular selves were immediately identified with their universality and committed the whole of the institution to a struggle against itself to suppress meaningful difference. For both institutions, self-comprehension took the form of self-destruction.

In the next chapter, I will pursue the project of forgiveness as the implications for an inductive consciousness that is for-itself but not yet in-and-for-itself; that is, we will follow forgiveness as its finds its universal identity, not in the institution of conscience but in the concept of experience.

CHAPTER FIVE

Induction and the Experience of Phenomenology

Introduction

In this chapter, my goal is to consolidate the position adopted by forgiving consciousness as knowledge, that is, as the singular act of transforming the range of its experienced otherness into the unity it commands as the universal self expressed in the institution of conscience.

The analysis of the need for experiencing consciousness to learn about the unity that organizes its experience led us to the need for it to become self-conscious, to learn how consciousness itself organizes experiencing. The initial form of self-consciousness, desire, is little more than the assertion that the singular self is the organizing principle of experience *tout court*. We learned from its experience that this assertion depended on its dissolution of what we knew to be determinate responses to experiencing made by singular consciousness, but mediated by experiencing itself. I argued that desire needed to learn how it has developed in response to experiencing, which required it to come to see the different forms of conscious life as a totality that is self-differentiated, self-mediating, and the object of its own act of inductive self-comprehension.

In the institution of slavery, the slave-self learned about an independently inductive singularity, but only because its dependence on its institutional and experiential history was concealed in the ruthless authority of the master, for whom singularity was something less than selfhood. In the last chapter, we followed the history of institutional life as it came to recognize its dependence on inductively singular selfhood in the institution of conscience. Conscience, we learned, is only fulfilled in the act in which the inductively singular self who appropriates its institutional universality in conscientious conviction takes responsibility for articulating that universality by forgiving the acts of others as legitimate expressions of universality.

In the sections that follow, I will first look at the way in which forgiveness as induction that is for itself recognizes that it belongs to the inductive singularity it forgives and inscribes its act of forgiveness in the universal unity of experience *phenomenologically*, by means of the systematic deduction of the forms it has inductively unified. In the next two sections, I will show how, as absolute knowing, phenomenology respects its own inductive development in the form of a transcendental deduction of the concept of experience that takes the form of a transcendental induction. That is, I will show how induction survives its role in helping us ascend to the summit and earns a permanent place in the deduction in which it culminates.

Forgiveness, Phenomenology, and Absolute Knowing

The analysis of forgiveness showed how it required an inductive approach to the forms of experiencing singularity expressed in the acts that it is compelled to regard as universally necessitated. To forgive is to know how these acts express the universality of the institutional context, and more important, to know how the context is the truth of the acts it expresses. In other words, the act of forgiveness knows the institutional context as the self-differentiating, self-mediating totality of the acts of conviction it sanctions.

In approaching experience inductively, the forgiving self investigates the experiencing individuals with whom it shares the context. It investigates its context as the universal self, and although it awaits the acts on which it depends for its realization, it is equipped with the logical principle of the totality that differs from itself and mediates itself through these actions. What this principle gives it is the framework within which all singular experiencing is comprehended.[1] What it enables it to do is to respect singular experiencing as self-determining, as expressing *its own* universal principle, which is at the same time the principle of forgiveness. What it brings to its inductive investigation then is the recognition that each singular self enacts its own situation from the necessity it recognizes and responds to as universal.

We have seen how this principle has been expressed through the history of developing consciousness, but forgiveness takes the form of the necessary anticipation of universality. What is missing, in the inductive standpoint that is now for-itself in the singular act of forgiveness is the recognition of itself as the culmination of the development of experiencing singularity. In acting as the universal self awaiting realization, the forgiving self is equally the moment of singularity, the experiencing self, necessitated by the institution of conscience and by the history of experiencing self-comprehension.[2]

To complete the act of forgiveness then requires that the singular self make explicit its own involvement in the institution it comprehends and that it know that institution as the concept of experiencing that is the proper object of its inductive investigation and what has given it the imperative to comprehend experiencing as such. To achieve this, however, requires that it has gathered all forms of experiencing and confirmed its own completeness by organizing them as the systematic expression of the concept.[3] It must gather the forms of experience and unify them as the necessary expressions of the totality of experiencing singularity, as the act of self-comprehension on behalf of the systematic totality to which it belongs.[4]

Phenomenology is the name for the inductive expectation that knows how to ask experiencing to show itself and that knows itself to be the self-comprehension of experiencing. It is inductive singularity which is in-and-for-itself, in belonging to that self-developing totality of which it is the articulation. That is, phenomenology is that which has gathered[5] together the ways of responding to experienced necessity as the response that has recognized the way that experience sanctions such gathering. Phenomenology involves the necessity of including its own method as the culminating moment of experiencing singularity and as that toward which all other forms have been striving.[6] It forgives the situated singularity that acts to the best of its abilities by showing exactly how its response was conditioned by the universal concept, and it shows how the same concept, now comprehended, was already there calling for its moments to be recognized as necessary.[7] Phenomenological analysis is therefore the moment of the concrete universality of singular selfhood *as* the moment of recognizing experiencing singularity in all its forms as concrete universality.

But precisely what the phenomenological analysis has to provide to complete the project of forgiveness is an account of these moments not only as the totality they are but as self-differentiated and self-mediating. To realize its forgiveness means to show how these moments arise and take their place in the whole. It isn't enough to view experiencing inductively and to posit a systematic whole. That systematic expression has to account for the differentiating of the concept from its moments as the elaboration of the concept in experiencing. Phenomenology as absolute knowing, or science, must provide the systematic self-expression in its experiential integrity.[8]

It is as a result then of the implications of its own project that it must realize itself as the phenomenology of phenomenology. That is, it must show how phenomenology is the form of experiencing sanctioned by experiencing itself as its complete self-comprehension. What is called Hegel's dialectical method is the demonstration of the dissatisfaction of experiencing with every other shape given to experiencing consciousness. The phenomenology of phenomenology has to show not only how each form of conscious life takes a rightful place in the totality of experiencing but how each in actualizing itself exposes itself to contradiction at the hands of the experiencing it purports to have comprehended. Not only must each shape demonstrate its belonging to the concept: it must equally show how it doesn't complete the concept, how it stands in need of further transformation.[9] Phenomenology, as the fulfillment of forgiveness, has to show itself to be the limit of that development by reconstructing it as the process itself, the process of each responding to the last and phenomenology responding to the whole.

In describing how the conceptual demands of the *Phenomenology of Spirit* are realized in a systematic science of dialectically related shapes of conscious life, I have shown just how the task of inductive singularity that is in-and-for-itself completes itself in the *deduction* of its own concept. It is important to see that its inductive work does subordinate itself to the unity that is to be expressed through the deduction of the concept it has developed from the forms of experiencing it has recognized. In showing how the concept of experiencing that serves as the condition for the possibility of each of these forms accounts for their emergence as real shapes of conscious life, phenomenological analysis shows how the concept itself requires these forms for its own realization. They belong to it as necessary and universal shapes, and only in its deductive deployment can we recognize and *know* that necessity and universality in its differences.

But precisely what our concept has shown us is that our science and the deductive method it employs

> does not exist before, and nowhere at all, till after the completion of its work of compelling its imperfect 'shape' to procure for its consciousness the 'shape' of its essence, and in this way to equate its *self-consciousness* with its *consciousness.*[10]

The community as religious presents us with experiencing in its own element and therefore expresses the fully-developed potential for science's realization. The existence of the religious community is prior to its actual self-recognition in science. The moments of conscious life, which as forms drive the potential to be realized *as* science, equally take their place first *in time.*[11] To the extent that the very existence of the science depends on induction then the demand that it respect and recognize that dependence *in its deduction* is legitimate.[12] Having seen how the science of experience respects its deductive completeness, let us turn now to the way in which the *Phenomenology of Spirit* respects its inductive origins.

The Unity of Induction and Deduction

One of the first gestures or expressions of conviction in the *Phenomenology of Spirit* is the claim that 'this is now'—it is the claim that experiencing immediately happens or can only be measured, or mediated, by time. Throughout the development of the science of experience, time is precisely what each of the immediate or natural forms of consciousness do not recognize. To the extent that the mediation of a posited universal would mean some role for experience and experience that is outside its (immediate) truth claim the forms of consciousness leading up to conscientious forgiveness have no use for time. It would be the measure of its confession of failure.[13]

And yet to the extent that such failure turns up over and over again it is reasonable to assume that time shows up too—as the measure of conscious experiencing that does not yet know itself in otherness but confronts it as an opaque and independent other. Time is what consciousness takes for order when it doesn't know itself as ordering.[14] Time belongs to the inductive development of the science of experiencing, because as we have seen the need for induction arises at just those times when consciousness confronts its experience without certainty or truth and has to learn from its experience how to put it together again. What it doesn't learn, at least until it has become phenomenological, is how it has depended on time, *on the experience it has not yet reconciled*, to learn what it takes to be necessary.

What distinguishes the phenomenological analysis and its deduction of the concept of experiencing is its recognition of its dependence on unreconciled experience, on what just seems to happen, to present to it the possibility for and the necessary path of development. The dialectical method which the concept of experience demanded to show how each form of conscious life takes its place in experiencing is equally employed to show how each form calls for its successor, by breaking down in experience what is required to progress.[15] That is, the dialectical method shows how each form takes its place and how each form is linked to the next and to the whole by induction. The recognition of its dependence on induction, on learning from experience when its own order has broken down, will take the form of restoring to time its role as the order that confronts induction and confronts it as unsatisfactory.[16] To recognize the necessity of those moments in the coming-to-be of science will mean telling the history of its coming-to-be, the inductive history of the stages of induction.

To tell such a history is to organize the deduction by inverting it—by showing how what it uses to organize itself is only a result. Such a deduction will have to confess that it is after the fact—Marx's reflection *post festum*[17]—and moreover, "that nothing is *known* that is not in experience."[18] It is to tell the story of the role of experiencing and time in the appearance of what needs to be known by the singular consciousness and of singular consciousness itself as the essential inductive moment in which experiencing consolidates its gains. The inductive development is both the way in which the subject, singular selfhood, becomes substance, or the in-itself to be comprehended, and substance becomes subject, or the determinate multiplicity unified and comprehended in its truth.[19]

Time, Hegel argues, is the only alienated order that captures the richness of experience and the succession of alternative alienated orders.[20] Indeed, it is precisely as the succession of alienated orders that the *Phenomenology of Spirit* situates time—as that "other" into which consciousness is driven out of its limited satisfaction. But it also is in this work that this other has to be recovered, because this other, as time or as experiencing, is the very concept whose development we are pursuing. Time, or experiencing that asserts itself against consciousness, not only cannot be excluded but is the very object to be comprehended. Each inductive act is, in this sense, trying to know what time is; only in phenomenology do we find that it belongs to the concept of experience as that appearance of the necessity of going beyond itself, of gathering back from time, from experiencing, a more comprehensive form of self-consciousness.[21]

Therefore, the transcendental deduction of the concept of experience is at the same time the transcendental induction of the concept of experience. The science shows in its deduction how it comes to be by singular consciousness learning from experience, from its limit as externalized, broken up, and contingent, what the concept is.[22] The transcendental induction is necessary to show that in sacrificing itself to this fragmentation it has gathered the concept that truly speaks from the phenomenon. The science shows how in just this case where precisely what is at stake is the concept of experience, experiencing must be the object, and induction must be the method.[23]

Time, and experiencing that has lost its apparent order, are absolute determinations of the science of the experience of consciousness, but only because it has sacrificed itself to them in order to learn from experience what they are. Having learned this, the science recognizes that disordered experiencing, as the *need* for inductive unification, belongs to it essentially as long as it is the concept of experience, the concept it had to bring back and the concept experience drove it to. Its transcendental deduction is a *recollection* of experiencing, a "comprehended history," of what happens according to experience; it is the transcendental induction that shows how the concept of experiencing is how and what it drives consciousness to recognize as itself, in its independence.[24]

Implications for Reading Hegel

The reading I have argued for here affects not only the conventional reading of the *Phenomenology of Spirit* but also the way we approach it in relation to Hegel's other works and those other works themselves. Let me conclude then by briefly pointing out some of these implications, not in a systematic way, but rather as indications for further study.

Hegel's *Phenomenology of Spirit* prepares us for his work in at least three ways. First, it provides for us the basis for understanding science as conceptual comprehension, both in the sense that, as absolute knowers, we have learned just what that comprehension entails in terms of the self-determining and self-differentiating totality that is the concept, and further, why that form of conceptual comprehension is what we mean when we speak of science. From the standpoint of the *Science of Logic*, to take the most compelling example, we can now see why the conceptual is both metaphysics, as the inner structuring and life of the real, and logic, or conceptual determination. Indeed, the primacy of the conceptual makes the *Science of Logic* a necessary second stage in our scientific education, precisely because "the development of this [spiritual] object . . . rests solely on the nature of the pure essentialities which constitute the content of logic."[25] In becoming what the *Phenomenology of Spirit* has taught us to be, our education now stands in need of further completion, to the extent that what we have been doing is examining scientifically something which wasn't our explicit concern when we set out. If the truth of our education to date is the discovery of "pure essentialities," then that must now form our explicit subject matter as scientists. We must learn how the conceptual order stands, not from the perspective of its emergence in and as the truth of our experiencing, but in its own right.[26]

The inductive argument of the *Phenomenology of Spirit* also prepares us for further scientific work, because it provides the conceptual basis for examining the various phenomena which have arisen within it. Perhaps the best example here is Spirit, which has emerged as the inner logic of cognition and been made explicit in the struggle for recognition. We can say, then, that the study of systems of Spirit is the study of the development of institutional forms of social life that are able to sustain and recognize the free rationality of the selves they define. It is the study of the actualization of the concept as the basis of social recognition. Again, we have been prepared for scientific analysis in our understanding of the method and concept of science and prepared here for the subject matter of Spirit, or systems of right.[27]

Finally, our inductive labors have prepared us to understand how the *Phenomenology of Spirit*, which culminates, as I have noted, in a "*begriffne Geschichte*," is at the same time a philosophy of history. Hegel's two lecture courses that address the concept of history, that is, world history and the history of philosophy, both depend on the conception of an experientially or temporally mediated conceptual development of the kind I have described here. The revolutionary nature of Hegel's historical epistemology is again put to work in the lectures on the history of philosophy, which provide an explicit description of the developmental continuity of Hegel's own thought with the thought of his predecessors. It is in this lecture course, more than any other place perhaps, that something similar to the form of inductive development I have described here is used as an interpretive model.[28]

Conclusion

I have argued here that Hegel's *Phenomenology of Spirit* develops inductively, or as the transcendental induction of the concept of experience, and I have shown why that must be. In the first chapter, we learned that experiencing in its simplest form is already organized in response to the demands experiencing poses from itself. To comprehend experiencing, the singular consciousness has to be driven to recognize something like experiencing as its source, and it has to recognize experience as the history of its own coming-to-be.

Just as we saw why self-knowledge develops inductively, or is learned from experience, we saw why this didn't become thematic in consciousness or self-consciousness as long as its operative principle was allowed to posit an *immediate* truth to experiencing. The inductive development of the concept of experiencing then is the result of experiencing driving consciousness toward a mediated or differentiated principle and the movement toward the recognition that this principle actively affects the truth consciousness wants to posit as immediate.

Finally, we learned that the various moments of the totality distinguished in this process mediate its truth only in that act of self-comprehension, in which the singular self knows the whole through the development that binds its parts. This knowledge, the absolute knowledge or the phenomenology that is able to provide the transcendental deduction of the concept of experience, must respect its dependence on what has been articulated inductively by organizing itself as the history of its own coming-to-be.

Notes

Introduction

1. Lectures on the History of Philosophy, vol. III, p. 176; Vorlesungen uber die Geschichte der Philosophie, p. 81.

References throughout this work will be to Miller's translation of the *Phenomenology of Spirit,* and they will be identified by paragraph numbers preceded by the letter M. Corresponding passages in the recent German edition prepared by Hans-Friedrich Wessels and Heinrich Clairmont will be cited by page number and preceded by W/C. In this case: M27, W/C 21: *"dies Werden der Wissenschaft uberhaupt, oder des Wissens."*

2. *Science of Logic*, p. 49.

3. These would include Robert Pippin's *Hegel's Idealism: The Satisfactions of Self-Consciousness* and Kenley Royce Dove's "Hegel's "Deduction of the Concept of Science.""

4. In spite of the care with which it approaches certain passages, Kenneth Westphal's *Hegel's Epistemological Realism seems open to the charge that it manipulates Hegel's thought into a very* contemporary, and perhaps un-Hegelian, controversy.

5. M26, W/C 19–21.

6. A recent example is George DiGiovanni's "Hegel's *Phenomenology* and the Critique of the Enlightenment," in which he argues that

Hegel objects to the manner in which Kant "stipulates those ideas a priori without asking just how, and why, one ever got to them."

7. This is stated quite clearly in M53: "[s]cience dare only organize itself by the life of the notion itself . . . [t]he determinateness which is taken from the schema and externally attached to a living thing, is, in Science, the self-moving soul of the realized content." W/C 39: "*Die Wissenschaft darf sich nur durch das eigne Leben des Begriffs organisieren; in ihr ist die Bestimmtheit, welche aus dem Schema ausserlich dem dasein aufgeklebt wird, die sich selbsts bewegende Seele des erfullten Inhalts.*"

8. It is in this sense that the *Phenomenology of Spirit* performs the task of a "phenomenology of phenomenology," called for by Merleau-Ponty in his *Phenomenology of Perception* (p. 365). That is, Hegel described phenomenologically the way in which experience itself demands that it be treated phenomenologically. On this theme, see the excellent work by Eugene F. Bertoldi, "Phenomenology of Phenomenology." David Levin also has raised the issues I am discussing here, in connection with Husserl, in "Induction and Husserl's Theory of Eidetic Variation." Levin rightly notices that phenomenology claims a unique access to experience and its comprehension and, through Hume's arguments against induction, claims that Husserl leaves himself vulnerable to charges of bad induction.

9. Induction is a word that turns up in interesting ways in his work, however, and a term that is linked to the kind of development I have in mind here. For example, the account of the inductive syllogism in the *Science of Logic* specifies that induction is the "syllogism of experience" (SoL p. 690; *Wissenschaff de Logik* p.338: "*der Schluss der Erfahrung*"). That is, it has implicitly formed the demand that only speculative philosophy can satisfy: the demand that universality be concrete, present in and as the experienced other. This same naively speculative element is identified with empiricism in the *Encyclopedia Logic*, where Hegel again praises the demand that what is known be here and now, calling it a demand that speculative philosophy could ignore only if it misunderstood philosophy, and shows how empiricism (rightly understood) is what drives us from mere perception to experiencing (see section 38 and additions). If Hegel ever seems dismissive of what gets called empiricism, it is because of its tacit rationalism: it claims to speak from experience, but it is rather a subjective philosophy of the understanding whose criteria are those of the rationalists, thus (paradoxically) formalistic and not empirical at all.

10. The word translated as education is *Bildung,* and while it would be overstating the case to claim that it translates as induction, the arguments I am making here suggest that such a move would not be as unlikely as it might seem. Rather, induction seems to be the energy or means of *Bildung,* which names the formative developmental process (the "process of origination") itself, as well as naming that social institution that defines itself as developing or transforming. Compare Hegel's extended use of the educational metaphor in M28, W/C 22–3.

11. M78, W/C 61.

12. The first chapter of Joseph Flay's *Hegel's Quest for Certainty* identifies very well the issues at stake for Hegel in refusing such philosophical privilege.

13. Sallis' best work on Hegel, in my reading, is his "Hegel's Concept of Presentation." Jay Lampert's "Husserl and Hegel on the Logic of Subjectivity" is one of the finest pieces of writing on phenomenology I have read and includes the most lucid and compelling definition of "dialectic" I have encountered in the literature.

14. Russon has given me access to his (as yet) unpublished doctoral dissertation, *Hegel on the Body,* and I cite it when appropriate below.

15. This last argument can be found in his "Hegel's "Freedom of Self-Consciousness" and Early Modern Epistemology."

1. *The Experience of Conscious Life*

1. Andrej Warminski's "Reading for Example: "Sense-certainty" in Hegel's *Phenomenology of Spirit*" catalogues the most prominent of these commentaries, focusing on those which isolate Hegel's suggestion that sensuous certainty write down its truth claim.

2. M90–1, W/C 69.

3. M90; W/C 69: "[*Unser Gegenstand*] *kann nicht anderes sein, als dasjenige, welches selbst unmittelbares Wissen . . . ist.*"

4. *Science of Logic* pp. 67–78, *WdL* pp. 51–64.

5. The distinction is a subtle one, because what is at stake, at least in part, in beginning the *Science of Logic* is the presupposition of the completion of the *Phenomenology of Spirit*; that is, the beginning of the former in some sense *already* means the latter. (One of the clearest accounts of this in the literature is Kenley Royce Dove's "Hegel's 'Deduction of the Concept of Science.'") The analysis Hegel carries out begins with a very general concern for initiating philosophical argu-

ments, then at times becomes determined by the specific nature of logical exposition and the specific relationship between a science of logic and the development of the scientific standpoint phenomenologically. In other words, the tension running between the logic of the beginning and the beginning of the logic makes any external application of the argument in this section problematic. This tension is often most, and not least, acute when Hegel addresses the argument of the *Phenomenology of Spirit* from the standpoint of the Science of Logic. My account below is drawn for the most part from the general remarks about the logic of beginnings.

6. The most helpful of these occurs in M24 (W/C 18), where Hegel contrasts his claim that science can only be realized as a system with the belief that particular philosophies are to be distinguished on the basis of their "basic proposition or principle" ("*Grundsatz oder Prinzip*"). Hegel's point is that the principle is self-falsifying if taken independently, because science must achieve a comprehensive and living actuality or be equal to that of which it is the science. By contrast, an asserted principle is empty and abstract.

7. Again, the remarks in M24 (W/C 18) suggest that the immediacy posited by sensuous certainty takes the form of a principle, which could never be the truth of experiencing in its vitality. The self-refutation of sensuous certainty is not the denial of immediacy but rather the denial that immediacy could take the form of a principle. The principle posited by sensuous certainty (something like the universal claim that "all experience is immediately") is necessarily over and against, and so mediated by, the experiencing of which it is supposed to be the *immediate* truth. As Quentin Lauer notes, in *A Reading of Hegel's Phenomenology of Spirit* (p. 50), Hegel shows that to be an empiricist in any meaningful sense, one will have to allow experience to tell its own story, and this is what sensuous certainty is not prepared to do. The positivist declarations of sensuous certainty have to give way, by virtue of the appeal to experience itself, to a more responsive intentionality.

8. See also M109, W/C 76, where Hegel expresses his astonishment that, given what we have seen of sensuous certainty, its basic claim is still advanced "as universal experience" ["*als allgemeine Erfahrung*"] in the form of a philosophical position or as the outcome of skepticism. Thus, I would argue that Joseph Flay (in the first chapter of his *Hegel's Quest for Certainty*) is mistaken when he attributes to sensuous certainty the status of "the natural attitude" that belongs to prereflective consciousness. As I argue below, perception is a much clearer form of ordinary

awareness, lacking the precision and perversity of sensuous certainty. These latter features animate Hegel's account of sensuous certainty, and it is precisely its "unnaturalness" that is at stake, its status as a *reflective* claim (or as a"philosophical proposition," in Hegel's analysis) about the necessity of avoiding reflection, as I will argue.

One important example of Hegel's contempt for a similar position advanced as a philosophical one can be found in his review of the work of Gottlob Schulze, published in Hegel's and Schelling's *Kritisches Journal der Philosophie* as *Verhältnis des Skeptizismus zur Philosophie, Darstellung seiner Modifikationen, und Vergleichung des neusten mit dem alten; in Erste Druckschriften*: pp. 161–211; *The Relationship of Skepticism to Philosophy* (in *Between Kant and Hegel*: pp. 314–354).

9. This is the significance of Hegel's remark in M24 (W/C 18) that immediacy in the beginning is only a principle or a *purpose* (Zweck).

10. In other words, the concern for an immediate beginning is misplaced. In his *Science of Logic*, Hegel argues that the concern for what comes first is the concern "not of *truth* but merely of *history*" (SoL 588; WdLII 226: "*nicht um die Wahrheit, sondern um die Historie*"), the concern of representational thinking for which the governing unity of development is time itself. To think the beginning that is really the end defies the temporal limits of representational thinking.

11. In M24 (W/C 18), Hegel describes the self-refutation of the principle as the demonstration that the principle which serves as the ground to a science is only a beginning and one that stands in need of fulfillment or realization.

The passage in the *Science of Logic* (SoL 689-92; WdLII 337–9) where Hegel describes the syllogism of induction as the syllogism of experience is significant in the context of the continuity of the beginning and the end and in the context of my argument later in this chapter, that is, that induction is the mediation that belongs to experience itself. Hegel's argument there, remember, is that logical induction has rightly identified the goal of a concept that is one with its instances, or which is self-differentiating, but lacks the appropriate standpoint for recognizing that identity. Nonetheless, its purpose remains constant, and it is the playing out or the realization of that purpose that makes it, I am arguing, the syllogism of experience.

12. I use the term *ontological* here to reflect the language of being with which sensuous certainty is always occupied. It knows what is; but

this is other than its knowing, so its knowing must be, etc. I don't mean to suggest that sensuous certainty is explicitly manipulating an ontology.

13. The translation of Hegel's "*Einzelne*" (M91, W/C 69) as "single item" introduces a word already burdened with unruly associations, although it is hard to defend an alternative precisely because any word other than those for the moments of space and time is already more than sensuous certainty can really admit. Hegel's *Einzelne* circumvents this by identifying the way the object of sensuous certainty is, in its singularity, already implicitly related to others by exclusion as its name. I shall refer for the most part to the activity of singling out, which suggests this negative self-relation without introducing new determinations and which has the added benefit of characterizing perceptual consciousness as well, thereby suggesting their continuity.

14. M 96, W/C 71.

15. Hegel's word is *zurückgedrängt*; M100, W/C 72.

16. M 96; W/C 71: "*gleichgültig*."

17. M 104; W/C 74: "*sich selbst gleichbleibende Bezeihung*."

18. Kenley Royce Dove, in "Hegel's Phenomenological Method," argues that a commitment to the truth of knowledge is inconsistent with Hegel's desire to refrain from positing the form knowledge must take. Instead, he suggests, Hegel wants us to "bracket" our concerns and pursue the descriptive analysis of ways of knowing with a kind of detachment. Dove's position echoes Findlay's claim that Hegel asks of us that we be like a "quietest saint" (*Hegel: A Reexamination*, p. 86) in our restraint. This approach to the argument is ruled out by Robert Pippin in "Hegel's Phenomenological Criticism"; Pippin argues, as I am here, that Hegel's "description" is instead a determined piece of transcendental argumentation and that our involvement is important at every moment. If one takes seriously the remarks in the preface about the universal individual prepared to take on the laborious education the *Phenomenology of Spirit* is supposed to be, detachment would seem to be counter-productive, at least in the sense that I will never see the point of, say, sensuous certainty, unless I share its goals and recognize its expression of necessity. There must be something I *want* to learn to do and that I take each of the shapes of conscious life, at least initially, to have worked out if I am to make sense of the argument in its integrity.

19. This is the argument made in the preface (M30–6; W/C 24–8) in order to distinguish the method of analysis which is proper to phenomenology and that practiced in natural consciousness, especially the under-

standing. The basis for the contrast is summarized in M36 (W/C 28), in terms of what I will describe below as the inductive method of Hegel's science: Its concern to examine each form of consciousness in terms of the experience it makes possible and to pursue only those possibilities for development which show up in the experience itself.

There is an important relationship between what Hegel is practicing here and Kant's description of "the skeptical method" informing his account of the "antithetic" of pure reason in the transcendental dialectic of the *Critique of Pure Reason* (A420–5, B448–53). According to Kant, the appropriate response to any apparently contrary position is to provoke conflict, not to side with the winner but to watch the controversy reveal as illusory the object dividing the combatants.

20. This is another way of saying that it has already contradicted its own truth claim in the very act of articulating it, which was part of my argument above and a difficulty Hegel draws our attention to in M91 ("All that it says about what it knows . . . "; [W/C 69: "*Sie sagt von dem, was sie weiß, nur* . . . "]) and again in M92 (" . . . which this certainty pronounces to be its truth . . . "; [W/C 70: " . . . *welches sie als ihre Wahrheit aussagt* . . . "].

21. There is an important argument concealed in the fact that the "default" context for sensuous certainty is time, or the now, which underlies Hegel's concern here (M105–7, W/C 74–5) in describing the first effort at pointing out. Time is the context in which experiencing 'just happens' for sensuous certainty, especially insofar as it is making a claim about its *own* experiencing. But experiencing is, like temporality itself, *already* mediated in the reflective claim of immediacy. The role of temporality is a theme which will recur in my argument and which will be treated in some detail in chapter 5, below, where I will characterize induction in-and-for-itself, or phenomenology, as "conceptualized history" (M808; W/C 531: "*die begriffne Geschichte*").

On the issue of time as the default context for consciousness, compare, for example, the passage in Hegel's lecture course on world history where he contrasts time, "the negative element in the *sensory world*," with "thought," which "is this same negativity . . . but it is the innermost form itself wherein everything that exists is, in principle, dissolved—and chiefly the finite being, the determinate form" (*Introduction to The Philosophy of History*; p. 80; *Vorlesungen über die Philosophie der Geschichte*, p. 101).

22. That is, the now that is pointed to is not the one intended by the certain individual, but neither is it the unity of the two in the face of which the individual shrinks back. The pointed-out now is determinate

because it is neither the one nor the other but the result of both, in Hegel's language, the negation of the negation. Hegel's reference here to an absolute plurality shows the extent to which the pointing out, when properly comprehended, really solves the problem of knowing.

23. M 107: "it is *something that is reflected into itself*, or a *simple* entity which, in its otherness, remains what it is: a Now which is an absolute plurality of Nows"; W/C 75: "*es ist eben ein in sich Reflektiertes, oder Einfaches, welches im Anderssein bleibt, was es ist; ein Itzt, welches absolut viele Itzt ist.*"

24. M 92; W/C 70: "*Eine wirkliche sinnliche Gewißheit ist nicht nur diese reine Unmittelbarkeit, sondern ein Beispiel derselben.*"

25. In other words, we have learned that experiencing demands the "synthesis of apprehension in intuition" and the "synthesis of reproduction in imagination," from Kant's transcendental deduction (*Critique of Pure Reason*, A98–110). This parallel has been noticed in a general way by Charles Taylor in "The Opening Arguments of the *Phenomenology*," and in just these terms by John Russon in "Hegel's 'Freedom of Self-Consciousness' and Early Modern Epistemology" and by Jean Hyppolite in *Genesis and Structure of Hegel's Phenomenology of Spirit*, (p. 105).

26. M113, W/C 80.

27. See M111 (W/C 79), where Hegel remarks that the movement of relating an aspect to its manifold is the proper object of perceiving consciousness. Compare this with the definition of cognition in M82 (W/C 64). It is important throughout the analysis of perception and understanding to recognize that *both* the detail (or what Hegel calls the property) and the thing are simultaneously constructions of perceiving consciousness: to take something as a detail implies that it belongs to some unity, and to identify such a unity entails that it is comprised of many such details. They are mutually determining moments of the logic of perception, or, they are both "properties" of perceiving consciousness. In other words, perception hasn't mistakenly unified what are really discreet sensible experiences; details like these only exist for perceiving consciousness.

28. Notice that already in the preface (M30–1, W/C 24–5) Hegel has announced that familiarity emerges as a sign of indifference, as an indication that consciousness is finished with its active relationship to experience and has taken on a complacent attitude toward its own activities.

29. In other words, perceiving consciousness doesn't necessarily pick out sensible qualities in the form of what Aristotle calls a "special" or "proper" object (*De Anima*, 418 a11 ff.), the kind of aspect appropriate to

each sense—colors, tastes, etc. Rather, it is a unified approach to otherness that can be so analyzed, or which offers itself to consciousness by means of such details, just as the unified object can. Jean Hyppolite makes a similar claim in *Genesis and Structure*, (p. 100). The important term for perceptual consciousness is *property* (*Eigensinn*), the name perception gives to the aspect which immediately belongs to some unity. Perception, for Hegel, implies no such dependence on specialization, which would presuppose a self-conscious and not a conscious relationship to its experienced otherness. In fact, the emergence of specialized senses in the dialectic of perception is taken by perception itself to be the way in which it interferes with the unity of its object; see M119, W/C 84–85. The key here is that there are two moments to its object, and it cannot account for *their* unity, which is of course its own unity.

30. Hegel's word for perception's relation to its signified universal is *gesetzt* (see, for example, W/C 80), which Miller translates with the verb "establish" (M113). The concept of *setzen* in this and in other places in Hegel's work (for example, in the dialectic of determinate being or *Dasein* in his *Science of Logic* [*SoL* 109–56; *WdL I* 95–146], to which the analysis of perception has important ties) suggests something more than the rather self-conscious tone that often accompanies the English verb "establish." The point is rather that perception, in taking something as a detail in this way, *posits* or logically determines a kind of object. It isn't something perception could ever be made aware of; as we have seen, perception cannot self-consciously take responsibility for its logical determinations, which must remain as presuppositions. The "posited" nature of its cognitive commitments are precisely what is at issue in the transition to the form of conscious life called the understanding, where what for perception is merely posited (*gesetzt*) becomes explicit as law—*Gesetz*. Compare also Hegel's account of positing reflection in the *Science of Logic*, pp. 400–02 [*Die setzende Reflexion, WdL II*, 15–17].

31. Described in M79, W/C 62, and again in M87, W/C 67–8.

32. M111: "That principle [the universal] *originated* for us, and therefore taking on perception is no longer, as was the case with sensuous certainty, based on what it appears to be, but is instead necessitated." (W/C 79: "*Jenes Prinzip ist uns entstanden, und unser Aufnehmen der Wahrnehmung daher nicht mehr ein erscheinendes Aufnehmen, wie der sinnlichen Gewißheit, sondern ein notwendiges.*") I have altered Miller's translation here to bring out the continuity between this very dense sentence and the description of how determinate negation operates within

the text in M 87 (W/C 67–8). I take the point here that sensuous certainty appeared to have immediate access to the truth, and we took it up on that basis. With perception, however, our choice of forms of conscious life cannot be made on the basis of what appears to be the case—*experiencing has told us* what our next form *must* be, namely, that form which meets the basic requirement experienced in our attempt to salvage sensuous certainty. The crucial term here is the verb *entstehen*, used in the introduction to describe the necessity that attaches to each new form of consciousness in the progression. Hegel's argument is that the necessity that perception arises here is to be found in the experience of sensuous certainty.

Quentin Lauer has a very different reading of this passage. In *A Reading of Hegel's Phenomenology of Spirit* (p. 55), he suggests that the sentence concerns not our phenomenological relationship to perception but a difference in the awareness proper to each of perception and sensuous certainty. This seems to depend on dropping the word *unser* from its role of modifying *Aufnehmen*.

33. My account of Aristotle here has been shaped by John Russon, with whom I first studied this text and who has characterized its "empiricism"—or what Russon calls Aristotle's "active empiricism"—in a manner that has deeply influenced my reading of Hegel. This account can be found in "Self-Consciousness and the Tradition in Aristotle's Psychology."

34. *An Pos* 100a3.

35. *Posterior Analytics*, Book II, chapter 19. Beyond the work of John Russon's cited above, there is at least one other excellent reading of Aristotelian epistemology that works with the broader definition of induction that I am arguing animates Hegel's work: L.A. Kosman's "Understanding, Explanation, and Insight in Aristotle's *Posterior Analytics*." Another interesting reading is the one offered by Martin Heidegger in "The Being and Conception of *Phusis* in Aristotle's *Physics*, Bk. I." Heidegger suggests that induction "means 'leading towards' that which comes into view insofar as we have previously looked *away*, over and *beyond* individual beings" (p. 226). Heidegger reads Aristotelian induction in terms of its uncovering organizing principles to which we are already committed in apprehending individual units but which are themselves concealed. This account of "seeing and making visible what already stands in view" (p. 226) is very similar to the description of phenomenology in *Being and Time*, and it is also arguably very close to what I

will define as induction in-and-for-itself, or phenomenology, in Hegel's science of experience.

Howard Kainz, in *Hegel's Phenomenology Part I*, suggests that the relationship between Hegel's *Phenomenology of Spirit* and his system can be explained by analogy to the role of induction in Aristotelian epistemology. Since he offers it as a way of making sense of the diminished role of phenomenology in the *Encyclopedia*, and since he leaves it undeveloped, it is hard to find common ground with my own argument, but it indicates (I think) that the broader (ancient) conception of induction still enjoys some currency today.

36. This is as true of the textbook accounts of induction offered, for example, by Brian Skyrms (in *Choice and Chance: An Introduction to Inductive Logic*) or Wesley C. Salmon (*Logic*) as it is of the more esoteric work of Hans Reichenbach (*The Rise of Scientific Method*), Jerrold J. Katz (*The Problem of Induction and Its Solution*), or Bertrand Russell (*The Problems of Philosophy*). Skyrms' language is typical: armed with certain "facts," we aim to make "rational expectations" or generalizations about the likelihood of all cases or instances sharing the determinate features of this one.

37. This form of induction is taken up in the experience of consciousness as observing reason, in section A, chapter five, of the *Phenomenology of Spirit*.

38. To paraphrase Hegel's remarks about so-called skepticism, this one-sided view of induction is itself one of the forms of consciousness we will encounter on the path itself: the understanding is Hegel's name for one attempt to explain experiencing in terms of concepts defined by their exclusion of the kind of volatility the understanding attributes to experiencing. The analysis of understanding consciousness is the object of my next chapter.

39. In the experience of observing reason, one of the first things we find is that it has forgotten its history (M233, W/C 158–9). The appeal to abstract rational categories as the goal of inductive inference finds its necessity in the experience of the unhappy consciousness in which singular self-consciousness finds itself subject to an inner necessity in its experiencing. Rational observation takes shape when consciousness identifies its rationality as the immediate authority discoverable in singular consciousness, then seeks to bring its experience into line with it. Hegel's complex analysis of the antagonistic relationship between experience and reason is the subject of John Russon's excellent account of the difficult

fifth chapter of Hegel's *Phenomenology of Spirit*, "Hegel's Phenomenology of Reason and Dualism."

40. In this respect, skepticism is merely self-conscious epistemology, or epistemology that has confronted its underlying dualism. To ask "What can I know?" is already to announce the difference between self and other that can only be bridged at the expense of the latter. The question then becomes: What constitutes the nature of skepticism? What are its responsibilities with respect to the fact that in being conscious it has already imposed a rule on what is other? These are the questions that we are to confront at the end of the next chapter.

Stephen Houlgate, in *Hegel, Nietzsche, and the Criticism of Metaphysics* (pp. 105–12), offers a more detailed account of Hegel's criticism of Hume and empiricism in general, describing the constitutive opposition that causes traditional empiricism to subvert its own project. Kenley Royce Dove, in "Hegel's Phenomenological Method," notices that Hegel's refusal to presuppose the determination of the conceptual unity of experience means that he "is far more "empirical" . . . than philosophers who call themselves "empiricists."" That is a helpful summary of my views here and throughout this work.

41. Paul Thagard argues that Hegel's logic of development is uniquely nonpositivistic, distinguishing Hegel's dialectical logic from other scientific methods. See his "Hegel, Science, and Set Theory." W. A. Suchting's "Hegel and the Humean Problem of Induction" describes Hegel's critique of rational observation in a similar light.

42. The first of these shows up in the repeated contrasts Hegel makes between the lifelessness of natural consciousness and specifically the understanding, for which concepts are dead and inert tools, and the science which takes its lead from the life of the concept in question "by giving determinateness an existence in its own element" (M32; W/C 26: "*daß es der Bestimmtheit in seinem Elemente Dasein gibt*"), or "in freeing determinate thoughts from their fixity so as to give actuality to the universal and impart to it spiritual life" (M33; W/C 27: "*durch das Aufheben der festen Gedanken das Allgemeine zu verwirklichen und zu begeisten*"; see also M50–4, W/C 37–41, where Hegel describes science as the "cunning" whose bringing the forms of consciousness to life seems to be abstaining from interference and yet is in fact forcing determinate shapes of knowing to express their own finitude and death). The second is the main element in Hegel's dialectical definition of experiencing, whose development is animated by the determinate negation I describe below.

43. I am referring here to the well-known discussion in M85, W/C 65–6, in which Hegel describes the self-regulating logic of experience in terms of its intrinsic propensity for self-correction.

44. Joseph Flay's analysis of this positing in terms of what he calls "praxical" or "pragmatic" presuppositions identifies many of the important issues at stake in my account but tends to assume a kind of conventional notion of experience—so he will, on occasion, distinguish knowing and having an experience, which seems a distinction Hegel is arguing is tenuous: Experience is necessarily cognitive.

45. M86; W/C 67: *"er ist über ihn gemachte Erfahrung."*

46. Notice that the inductive development of a new principle preserves the prior one because it is the difference between what the prior principle sanctioned and what erupts in experience as unreconciled by that principle that the induction unifies.

Abigail L. Rosenthal, in "A Hegelian Key to Hegel's Method," argues that the need to overcome the respective crises that erupt along the path of development is not something alien to consciousness and only smuggled in by the scientist: [i]t is 'necessary' that the problem be solved, because if it is not solved, we will still be faced with the problem . . . [w]ere there no such necessity of finding solutions, action would have no motive and inaction no price" (p. 210).

47. This is the sense George Schrader gives to what he calls "empirical" philosophy, in "Hegel's Contribution to Phenomenology"—namely, that it "makes direct use of empirical materials" (19) rather than adopting an external relation to an experience predefined and "only indirectly confronted" (18). He argues that Hegelian phenomenology reveals the continuity between empirical and speculative (which he reads as "observational") philosophy, in its recognition that experiencing is self-reflective, and that self-development is "the essential logic of experience" (p. 20). He pursues this theme with respect to what he calls a tradition of "Continental empiricism," running from Kant to Husserl and beyond. He is, however, critical of what he sees as the antidialectical tendency in Husserl's phenomenology, which he attributes to Husserl's Kantian concern with the thing itself and the legacy of Descartes, and he is equally concerned with its echoes in Sartre, to whom he attributes a Cartesian dualism. His argument throughout is that Hegel's "empiricism" is precisely what phenomenology ought to have at its core: the self-conscious struggle with those phenomena in which one is implicated, rather than an external meditation on posited fundamental truths.

48. Compare Hegel's remark at M36: "[c]onsciousness knows and comprehends only what falls within its experience" (W/C 28: "*[d]as Bewußtsein weiß und begreift nichts, als was in seiner Erfahrung ist*").

John Dewey, a philosopher with admitted Hegelian and Aristotelian prejudices, is equally adamant that "[t]he act of knowing . . . is always inductive" (*Experience and Nature*, p. 285). Dewey anticipates the criticisms leveled against both the rationalist defense of induction in the form of probability theory and the rationalist attack against induction by Max Black in *Language and Philosophy*: namely, that the so-called "problem of induction" stems more from the rigid categories of abstract rationality that are imposed on experience than from the mode of thinking it represents. Both Dewey and Black speak of the "problem of *deduction*" of abstract categories, that is, their abstractness, their inability to say anything about experience. Dewey not only claims, as Hegel will, that abstract rationality is itself "inductive," or emerging as the necessary way of unifying a kind of experience, but also that "[t]here is only one mode of thinking, the inductive, when thinking denotes anything that actually happens" (ibid. p. 285).

49. For those forms of conscious life that are founded on the exclusion of mediation by experience or that take the form of what I will describe in the next chapter as "natural" consciousness, this involves what Hegel describes as "death" or self-inflicted violence. See M32, W/C 25–6, and M80, W/C 62–3.

50. Of course, the only adequate basis of evaluating the role of experiencing will be at the completion of its self-comprehension, thus in a sense the appropriate issues have not yet fully emerged. Nonetheless, it is worth mentioning here that emphasis on the role of experiencing in Hegel's text is not a common feature among the commentators. They are roughly divided on this point into those who believe that the *Phenomenology of Spirit* is a closed text and one which does not admit experiential contingency or self-determination in any useful way, and those who believe it may, but not in the sense Hegel intended. The first of these groups is perhaps the largest and certainly the most influential, made up of all those who object in one way or another to what is commonly called the methodology of the text. As might be imagined, this is a diverse group. Perhaps its most notorious member is Kierkegaard, whose critical remarks on Hegel's thought are founded on its alleged exclusion of the moment of radical singularity, the existing "I." Another influential critic is Heidegger, whose thinking is deeply engaged in a more or less

explicit "*Auseinandersetzung*" with Hegel's. Perhaps the most representative of his writings on Hegel is the essay "*Hegels Begriff der Erfahrung*," in *Holzwege* (published singly in English as *Hegel's Concept of Experience*). Heidegger's concern there stems from his understanding of the history of metaphysical thinking and, more specifically, from the obsession expressed by veridical forms of thinking for mastery and control, or exploitation. In "*Hegel's Begriff der Erfahrung*," he argues that the *Phenomenology of Spirit* is driven not by an increasing sensitivity to the demands of experiencing but by an increasingly articulated mastery of self-presencing. Heidegger finds in Hegel's text the self-manifestation of the infinite form of object-oriented consciousness, the consciousness of controlling things that appears in metaphysics as will—the text, for Heidegger, is the self-manifestation of self-willed willing.

The most intriguing work in the group is Adorno's, who disagrees with Hegel's own description of what happens, but who agrees that experience is doing something here. His essay "*Erfahrungsgehalt*" (in *Drei Studien zu Hegel*) rejects Heidegger's reading as having trivialized the role of experience, of history, in the mediation of Hegel's argument. Although Adorno argues that there is much more to be made of the movement of history than one can find in Hegel's work, he claims Hegel points the way to its recovery.

51. One of the most explicit passages to deal with the relationship between the "first" or "historical" development is M28–9, W/C 22–4.

52. Hegel's description of the "universal individual" ("*das allgemeine Individuum*") throughout the preface (see especially M26–30, W/C 19–25), as both the figure whose development we are recollecting and the figure who undertakes the project of recollection, is the characterization of who "we" are—namely, those readers who are thinkers, who are prepared to pursue the development by invigorating each form of conscious life and experiencing the need for a determinate transition.

53. Martin DeNys' "Self-Consciousness and the Concept in Hegel's Appropriation of Kant" characterizes the double aspect of the logic of the *Phenomenology of Spirit* very well: "Method for Hegel is the process through which thought recovers the self-relation and autonomy it has already achieved in the Concept and the fully developed Idea, by relating itself to its own other" (p. 155).

54. M109: "That is why the natural consciousness, too, is always reaching this result and experiencing what is true in it but just as often only to forget it again, thus to start the movement again from the begin-

ning" (my translation); W/C 76: "*Das natürliche Bewußtsein geht deswegen auch zu diesem Resultate, was an ihr das Wahre ist, immer selbst fort, und macht die Erfahrung darüber; aber vergißt es nur ebenso immer wieder, und fängt die Bewegung von vorne an.*" I have altered Miller's translation to reflect a very important issue here. The phrase "learning from experience" typically means something like "learning the hard way," or having to experience a truth rather than anticipating it on the basis of present knowledge. This is what the German phrase "*Erfahrung machen*" suggests as well, and it would be a good translation for most all of Hegel's uses of the phrase (another important one comes in M168) *except* here, because what is at stake is a form of consciousness that precludes learning from experience at all. The point of the experiencing/forgetting conjunction is to describe the inability of natural consciousness to survive the recognition of its own contradictory claim and its intrinsic resistance to development. This will be a crucial issue in the next chapter, especially in the experience of desiring self-consciousness.

55. In fact, deduction is present in two forms throughout the text: first, as the transcendental deduction of the concept performed by the scientist in the sense specified above, then again in what we contribute to the text by animating each new rule. That is, the experience of each rule that we are responsible for bringing to life is, in the sense of Aristotle's practical syllogism, a deduction of the rule mediated by the individuals it has specified. Like the confirmation of deduction which masquerades as induction in science, we are trying to confirm the rule or to deduce from it the experience it entails.

56. As John Sallis argues in "Hegel's Concept of Presentation," "the directedness [of the scientific presentation], rather than imposing the transition on the matter, only frees the transition that is already in the matter itself, only regathers what is already itself implicitly gathered, or, more precisely, lets it show itself as self-gathering" (p. 156). I will return to the relationship between induction and "gathering" in my final chapter.

57. One of the clearest accounts of this reciprocal entailment of induction and deduction as the dialectic of the scientific concept of experience can be found in Jay Lampert's "Hegel and Husserl on the Logic of Subjectivity." Although Lampert doesn't use the term *induction*, his description of dialectical development makes clear both how experiencing "activates" the development of the transcendental structures of selfhood and how the scientific standpoint requires what he calls a "backward reference" to that process of activation.

58. And in this sense, because we have the inductive movement of consciousness "for itself," we are prototypes of the phenomenologists we will become in absolute knowing.

59. It is not unique in this respect, that is, in being dependent on a unification of what has gone before it; this is true of each and every form of conscious life.

60. M87; W/C 68: "*der dem Bewußtsein, ohne zu wissen, wie ihm geschieht, sich darbietet, ist es, was für uns gleichsam hinter seinem Rücken vorgeht.*"

61. Of course, the unity that these details point to is perceiving itself; the failure to recognize this is what precipitates the crisis of the understanding, which I will examine in my next chapter.

62. This is the way that perception runs into trouble, and it is just another way of saying what I suggested above: that perception posits a relation between sensible details, or properties, and unities, or things, which cannot ever be defended on the basis of the experience perceiving makes possible. No sensible detail that is taken to imply a unity can ever by itself identify one unity and not another. As I argued above, the sensible detail really implies sensibility itself, the unity of all sensible details as employed in meaningful ways by the individual consciousness.

63. This twofold determination of the property, that it be distinguished from and in the same way related to others, echoes Hegel's description in the introduction (M82, W/C 64) of the cognitive intentionality of all forms of conscious life. In other words, at this stage in its gradual emergence from the object-orientation of natural consciousness, the individual consciousness assigns to the property its own role of actively negating its objects.

64. Notice that in the previous section I identified the crisis in sensuous certainty as the recognition that it had two objects on its hands: what it thought it had and what its acts have shown to be the result of its way of acting. Also, the resolution of that crisis was said to consist in our unifying those two as a new cognitive stance, which is what the second claim I am treating here does.

65. Once again, the crucial moment of crisis in a shape of consciousness is realized: what it took to be true, the way things really are, is reduced to a product of its attention. In Hegel's words, "What first appeared as the object sinks to the level of its way of knowing it" (M 87; W/C 67: "*Was zuerst als der Gegenstand erschien, dem Bewußtsein zu einem Wissen von ihm herabsinkt*").

66. This prior commitment was indicated in the initial act of perception. Perception claims to identify the property which leads it to recognize one thing, but the very act of picking out a property presupposes the unity of the determinate thing.

2. *Understanding, Desiring, and Death*

1. This is what we have seen in the experience of perception: that what unifies the two moments is the positing relation-through-difference which is the act of the perceiving consciousness. But, as Hegel notes, we are not yet at a form of consciousness which has experienced the need to see itself in experiencing and which takes its unifying principle as a principle of objectivity alone; M132, W/C 93.

2. One example of this is Michael Baur's "Hegel and the Overcoming of the Understanding," which attempts to liberate Hegel's analysis of "scientific consciousness" (p. 144) from the outdated Newtonian paradigms it employs. Baur's otherwise interesting analysis is weakened by his claim that in this chapter "consciousness moves from the perspective of common sense to that of modern science" (p. 144). This introduces into his reading a premature (from the perspective of the experience we are examining) emphasis on self-consciousness, an almost inevitable result given the methodological preoccupations of modern science. For example, Baur states that "relations grasped by the Understanding are supposed to hold for all possible observers, that is, under all possible observational contexts" (p. 148), and goes on in a footnote to compare this to the normative aspirations of empiricism. The commitment to what every experiencing individual ought to recognize as the truth of their experience is characteristic of the form of consciousness Hegel calls "reason"; the experience of the understanding is preparing us for self-consciousness, but as Hegel notes early on, its truth has *objective* significance—that is, its commitment is to what every appearance ought to recognize as its truth, which is the normative thrust of its laws of the natural world.

Both Gadamer (in "Hegel's 'Inverted World'") and Hyppolite (in *Genesis and Structure of Hegel's Phenomenology of Spirit*) read the chapter as primarily concerned with issues arising directly from natural science.

3. Compare M50, W/C 37, where terms drawn from traditional epistemology (like subject and object) are included with the scientific

examples. Baur (cited above) notes the relevance of the themes of traditional epistemology (p. 148) and rightly identifies Humean and Kantian issues as what are under discussion here, but mistakenly views modern science as what Hegel has at stake in all three.

4. Remember that, in the experience of perceiving, citing one property as the sign of some thing meant that one had to posit the multiplicity of properties, over and above the one cited, that were entailed in the idea of the thing as a unity of many properties. The problem was that there was no way to secure the unity of the thing on the basis of properties, because any one property demanded that we posit an indefinite or indeterminate "more," whereas we wanted just as many as belonged to, or were proper to, this one thing.

5. Both Hyppolite and Lauer in their accounts of the argument here emphasize the continuity between perception and the understanding, a continuity made most pronounced in Hegel's text by his conflating the two terms (see M131, W/C 81) at the close of the chapter on perception. I am trying to account for that continuity in terms of the kind of genetic process Hegel is concerned to describe.

6. Hegel warns us that the task facing the unity that the understanding is committed to, the unity *between* unity and multiplicity, is to preserve the very difference its predecessor found an untenable alterity. The name Hegel gives this unity, the "unconditioned universal" ("*unbedingt Allgemeine*"), suggests that it is already collapsed: as "*unbedingt*," or literally un-thinged, the universal adopted by the understanding expresses the primacy of the unity over and against its multiple terms.

Neither English translator manages to convey an important theme running throughout the chapter that is developed in Hegel's warning in the opening paragraph. The German text (W/C 93) runs: "*Dies Unbedingte wäre nun selbst wieder nicht anders, als das auf eine Seite tretende Extrem des für sich Seins, wenn es als ruhiges einfaches Wesen genommen würde, denn so träte ihm das Unwesen gegenüber.*" Both Miller and Baillie lose the participial form of the verb *treten* in their translations, which means they lose Hegel's point that, even in attempting to relapse into a static unity, the understanding must be *moving*, or stepping, moving over and against the dynamic unity to which it is committed. This is an important part of the analysis of the understanding, first because it shows us how the understanding, like its predecessors, exhibits in its behavior a commitment to a more complex project than the one it claims for itself. The other concern here is that Hegel uses forms of the verb *treten* throughout the chapter to flag just those occasions when the understanding continues to develop the deeper project even in recoiling from it. Evasive footwork becomes a running theme in the chapter devoted to the form of conscious life which constantly retreats to a complacent stance. This issue of movement is also our concern, because as Hegel warns us, if the understanding stands to one side, we must "step in" for it (M133, W/C 94: "*an seine Stelle zu treten*").

7. Again, this seems to speak against the "quietist saint" reading adopted by Findlay and developed by Dove.

8. M134: "The result was the unconditioned universal, initially, in the negative and abstract sense that consciousness negated its one-sided notions and abstracted them: in other words, it gave them up." W/C 94: "*Das Resultat war das unbedingt Allgemeine, zunächst in dem negativen und abstrakten Sinne, daß das Bewußtsein seine einseitigen Begriffe negierte, und sie abstrahierte, nämlich sie aufgab.*" The point here is that in bringing them together as thoughts, removed from the experience of perceiving, the understanding has removed them from (or "given up") their tenuous relation to the experience of sensible detail and already implicitly assigned thought responsibility for their truth.

9. M134, W/C 94.

10. The back-and-forth of ordinary consciousness then has attained the dignity of a physical process.

11. M 136, W/C 95–6.

12. M141, W/C 99–100.

13. M139, W/C 98.

14. M140, W/C 98–9.

15. M144, W/C 101–2.

16. M143, W/C 100–1; M147, W/C 103.

17. Again, the immediate antithesis takes shape as a sign that induction is still in-itself.

18. It is important to see that appearance doesn't name simply the field of determinate things but the relation between that field and its unity. It is the difference between these moments that is appearance, the difference that is experienced by sensuous certainty and perception. Compare M143, W/C 100–1, where Hegel distinguishes appearance as the middle term in the syllogism of the understanding as a "vanishing," that is, as the alternation of the reciprocally determined moments.

19. M148–9, W/C 103–5. What the phrase "the law of force" suggests is precisely the fact that the universality the understanding has

posited as the concept of force demands, or posits, its own difference. (This is better captured in German, of course, because the word *Gesetz*, which translates as law, is closely related to the past participle of the verb *setzten*, which translates as "to posit.") This is a complex relationship, as we will see, and one in which is contained all the subsequent themes in the experience of the understanding as well as all the prior ones. The point here is that in repeatedly positing unity in the face of difference, the understanding has been driven to a form of unity or universality that forces it to readmit difference, as the difference belonging to universality itself. This is what will ultimately present itself as the inverted world: the necessity that any universal generate or posit as its own the differences upon which it depends as unity.

Martin J. De Nys' careful reading of this chapter ("Force and the Understanding: the Unity of the Object of Consciousness") falters on this crucial issue. His gloss of universal difference, "difference which is indifferent to itself" (p. 61), addresses only the negative sense in which as universal, difference is abstracted from the many specific differences which have emerged in the experience of the understanding. This is certainly important to the crisis in which the understanding ultimately finds itself, but it overlooks the important contribution made by the installation of a universal that must be self-differentiating in principle.

20. M149; W/C 105: "*dem beständigen Bilde der unsteten Erscheinung.*"

21. M150; W/C 105: "*unbestimmt viele Gesetze.*"

22. Resorting to the positing of one, universal law, or the assertion that all events are law-governed, the understanding reveals itself to be closely related to a kind of inductive enterprise often advanced and attacked by epistemologists and philosophers of science. In the name of unifying empirically events defined by their intrinsic lack of unity, some have argued that the most basic presupposition must be that there is some regular or uniform behavior exhibited by any event. John Stuart Mill, in *A System of Logic*, argues that the lawlike uniformity of nature "is the fundamental principle, or general axiom, of Induction" (224). He states that it is *not* an imposed axiom, but itself one resulting from induction. David Hume is quite well-known for having targeted the presupposition of the legitimacy of translating the discreet moments of experience into the language of conceptual uniformity in his *Treatise on Human Nature*. Gottlob Frege, in *Die Grundlagen der Arithmetik*, also takes a much harsher view of positing lawlike behavior. He argues that induction depends on positing

the expression of laws in the events it observes, noting that without this, "*ist die Induction nichts weiter als eine psychologische Erscheinung*" (p. 4).

Our analysis of the understanding shows us that both views have identified a part of the truth. The need to posit the uniformity of what appears to us is something that does arise from or find its justification in our experience. On the other hand, to resolve what appears to us in the form of a general proposition only carries the weight of truth if we have already posited that such a universalizing or unifying term can in fact stand as the truth of what is experienced as a multiplicity.

23. M151, W/C 106.

24. M152-3, W/C 107-8.

25. This is the issue that Nelson Goodman raises in trying to establish his "new riddle" of induction, namely that the epistemological problem for induction is not whether we can justify any prediction about future experience but whether we can distinguish between contingent and lawlike predictions. For Goodman, there is in the observed objective field no such basis for distinction, thus all induction is essentially contingent.

Precisely what the experience of the understanding has shown us is that, abstracted from experiencing itself, attempts to comprehend the objective world "on its own terms" force us to make distinctions that ultimately show themselves to be unwarranted. Goodman's concern for lawlike predictions is one of these. Lawlike behavior is the behavior of experiencing individuals in comprehending experience, not of objectified and predicated aspects themselves. Goodman, who seeks to replace Hume's claim that induction is problematic because it is only a habitual form of experiencing, overdetermines as proto-scientific the manner in which induction is said to occur, and thereby misses Hume's somewhat subtler point that induction somehow belongs to the way we experience in spite of its apparent difficulties.

26. M156, W/C 110–1.

27. The issue here is clearly the Kantian dualism of thing-as-experienced and thing-in-itself. Hegel's argument here is that the difference is posited by experiencing, and that the thing-in-itself therefore belongs to experience, or arises from within it. The crucial claim in the argument is that the understanding can, if driven to it, experience this difference as its own.

28. The analysis here focuses on paragraphs M166–77 (W/C 120–7). I am indebted to John Russon's analysis of the concept of life in *Hegel on the Body* and to a discussion group organized to read this section

of the *Phenomenology of Spirit* (and the parallel analysis of life in the *Science of Logic*), which included Kenneth Cheung, David Morris, and John Russon.

29. It will become clear that I disagree with Peter Preuss' suggestion (in "Selfhood and the Battle: The Second Beginning of the *Phenomenology*") that the transition from the experience of the understanding to desire is a "deviation from the program of the Introduction." Preuss, whose declaration that this claim that there is a breakdown in internal logic is "too obvious" to warrant defending, apparently includes in his sense of the "program" the bizarre prescription that each and every stage in the text's development *literally* write its own entry (p. 75). Preuss seems most alarmed by the regressive character of desire—after affirming as self-evident that it is an impossible transition, he goes on to complain (n. 4) that babies desire, and they don't develop from "physicists."

The key to the transition is well captured by a remark of H. S. Harris.' In his response to a paper of Kenley Dove's ("Comment on Phenomenology As Systematic Philosophy"), Harris argues that "[t]he problem of Logic is not simply "What is determinacy?," but rather "What is self-determinacy?"" (p. 44). Although Harris indicates that this clarifies the transition from logic to nature, it does equally well accounting for the transition here. Consciousness has asked, in the understanding, what is the law that governs things? Having given itself the answer, "I am," it needs to ask how. Desiring self-consciousness is the answer that involves recasting the laws of the understanding as functions of the singular self who makes this discovery of self-legislation. Babies do experience desire, and there is no question that the initial form of self-consciousness is "infantile" in many (nonpejorative) respects. Just as children learn the limits of selfhood through the limits on desire, so too will the universal individual whose education we are following. This reading of the transition, that it marks the move from objective verification to social limits as the criterion for knowing, is articulated and defended in Robert Pippin's "You Can't Get There From Here: Transition problems in Hegel's *Phenomenology of Spirit*."

30. M166, W/C 120.

31. M167, W/C 121–2.

32. M167, W/C 120–1. The experience of desiring self-consciousness is primarily occupied with the disparity between the necessity of the determinate object for its desiring and its inability as desire to recognize that necessity, or to respect it.

33. That is, it presupposes the experience of the nonreflective consciousness we have called perception, or the understanding, as that which it will show to be really self-consciousness.

34. M168: "([S]elf-consciousness) is the unity *for which* the infinite unity of the differences is; (life), however, *is* only this unity itself, so that it is not at the same time *for-itself*." (W/C 122: "*([D]as Selbstbewußtsein ist) die Einheit, für welche die unendliche Einheit der Unterschied ist; (das Leben) aber ist nur diese Einheit selbst, so daß sie nicht zugleich für sich selbst ist.*").

35. Hegel alludes to this incapacity for self-development in M171 (W/C 123–5) and to its dependence on another to recognize it as a unity in M172 (W/C 125); it is to both of these paragraphs that I am referring in what follows. I will return, in section (c) below, to the necessity that self-consciousness develop its recognition of life.

36. Anything that doesn't fall within the limits posited by the living thing of what will count for it as food makes no difference at all, not even an apparent one. This is another way of describing life in terms of desire: whatever it doesn't unconsciously need for its self-maintenance doesn't even exist. Rousseau uses the nonexistence of what lies outside of its posited object to distinguish between the starving animal that sits obliviously on top of food *we* know it could receive nourishment from, and the human, who has the power of freedom from mere instinct. His point, like Hegel's here, is that the merely natural is incapable of learning or developing a sense of what it is doing, even when that means its very survival.

37. John Russon's account of Life, in *Hegel on the Body*, works through the logic of differences posited as already overcome in much greater detail than I do here, and my account is indebted to his.

38. M169, W/C 122-3; M171, W/C 123–5. The abstract negation of life is an important expression of what Hegel will later identify as the form of conscious life called skepticism. The constitutive activity of life involves recognizing determinate objects and then undoing those determinations as apparent differences within the unity of the living being. The skepticism of traditional epistemology is, in one sense, life for-itself, or desiring self-consciousness as a reflective activity. I will return to this in section (c) below.

John McCumber, in *The Company of Words*, identifies the abstract negation we have seen in both the understanding and life as "one which, like death, does not preserve what it negates" (p. 147). I will be arguing for a view like the one expressed by McCumber in this and the next chapter.

For these reasons, I am extremely sympathetic to the view advanced by Kojève in "L'Ideé de la Mort dans la Philosophie de Hegel," that Absolute Knowledge and the self-conscious realization of death as pure annihilation are one (p. 540), and to his general claim that the *Phenomenology of Spirit* is a work about death.

39. M78; W/C 62: "*in der Tat dessen unfähig ist, was es unternehmen will.*"

40. M77, W/C 60.

41. M79, W/C 62.

42. Charles Taylor, in "The Opening Arguments of the *Phenomenology*," glosses natural consciousness as "commonsense" (p. 157), as does Robert Pippin in *Hegel's Idealism* (p. 95). It is no accident, I think, that both authors interpret the argument of the *Phenomenology of Spirit* explicitly (and one-sidedly) in terms of a transcendental deduction, where the role of experiencing I am arguing for is moot. From this standpoint, natural consciousness is simply 'not-yet science,' and moreover implicitly identified with the forms of object-oriented consciousness we already have examined. As I will go on to argue, natural consciousness is a continuing presence over the course of the text.

Kenley Dove, in "Hegel's Phenomenological Method" (p. 624), identifies natural consciousness with the individuality of the consciousness under investigation, which erases the specific logic I will describe below, yet at the same time recognizes that the term *natural* is construed by Hegel in terms much broader than common sense, encompassing the full range of shapes described by the text, and that it marks the self-identity at stake in losing one's grip on making sense of things. A very different account of what Hegel means by natural can be found in Lauer's A *Reading of Hegel's Phenomenology of Spirit*: He takes it to refer to what is biologically given, then opposes it to the spiritual, a move that has the unfortunate consequence of precluding "natural" expressions of Spirit, which Hegel could hardly do given what we will see is his analysis of *Sittlichkeit*.

43. At least two important commentators have developed the sense in which natural consciousness is the resistance to development, and as resisting, equally the key factor in development. Werner Marx, in *Hegel's Phenomenology of Spirit*, argues that natural consciousness "binds" the individual to its situation and thereby "determines" the situation without seeing itself as doing either. Marx's account also parallels mine in his suggestion that natural consciousness is with us throughout the *Phenomenol-*

ogy of Spirit. John Sallis defines natural consciousness, with Hegel, as "the I's taking itself to be outside the absolute," and attributes to it the "serious opposition, resistance, tension" that troubles the development of scientific knowing ("Hegel's Concept of Presentation" p. 149).

44. The clearest examples of this are in the first two cases, in part because with the understanding we have taken over its concept almost from the beginning, to bring out the differences implicit in its conception of force. In the case of sensuous certainty, Hegel describes its dissolution of the results which ought to compel it to advance in M109, W/C 76. Perceptual consciousness' inability to develop is characterized not as a dissolution of what it has experienced but as a kind of schizophrenic alternation between first one, then the other, of its constitutive moments.

45. This would explain the tension between natural consciousness as what develops, and as what is opposed to developing: as developing, it is still learning, or still inductive in-itself, and not yet able to recognize the relationship between its principle and its experience, thus again is opposed to exposing itself to experiential instability.

46. M79, W/C 62.

47. M168, W/C 122.

48. This is what leads Hegel to identify desiring self-consciousness as "the motionless tautology of: 'I am I'" (M167; W/C 121: "*die bewegungslose Tautologie des: Ich bin Ich*").

49. And, in some sense, the death of conscious life will remain a consequence of self-consciousness. The goal is to have self-consciousness take responsibility for these deaths, to restore them as sacrifices, and not to run through them in abstract slaughter. For one of the best accounts of this important distinction in Hegel's conception of the relationship between life and self-consciousness, see Bataille's "Hegel, Death, and Sacrifice."

50. M79, W/C 62.

51. M78, W/C 60–2.

52. If the understanding saw its immediate identity as objectivity, desiring self-consciousness merely reverses that one-sidedness and proclaims the truth of subjectivity.

The experience of those forms of conscious life which take subjectivity as their truth is described in chapter 4 of the *Phenomenology of Spirit*, and it culminates in the experience of the unhappy consciousness, which learns that its own subjectivity is already more than merely "mine"; it commands all "subjects" as such and takes the form of laws. I will examine the emergence of that social and law-governed self-consciousness in my fourth chapter, below.

53. M175, W/C 126.

54. M168, W/C 122; M175, W/C 126.

55. M176, W/C 127.

3. *Induction and the Experience of the Singular Self*

1. I have so far identified inductive development in terms of the transformation of the categories whose positing makes experience possible. Those commentators who, I think, have recognized in some implicit way the significance of learning and education in this chapter, tend toward using this term, including Lauer (in *A Reading of Hegel's Phenomenology of Spirit*, p. 107), and Kojève (in *Introduction a la Lecture de Hegel*, p. 34). Transformation, of course, matters here because it is what the slave learns it is capable of—that is, it can transform not only the world, but through the world, its awareness of itself. Robert Williams, in *Recognition*, provides a very helpful account of what the slave "comes to see," which places emphasis on the developmental or educational features I am describing here. Williams' argument also is especially clear on the role experience, or what he calls "empirics," has to play in the story of institutional development that commences in this section. On my reading, however, that role isn't exclusive to the explicit struggle for recognition, but has been with us all along.

2. I will be examining paragraphs M194–196 (W/C 134–5) here in detail.

3. M186–9, W/C 129–32. I will analyze these paragraphs, which constitute the transition from desiring self-consciousness to slavery, in section (3) below.

4. M194, W/C 134. This is a crucial component in the slave's emerging self-consciousness, because what really drives its acting is its fear for its own life—its work in transforming the natural world is something that it sees as its own. I will return to this transcendent lord and the significance of the slave's having internalized it in the next section of this chapter.

5. The difference between fear and service is that the former, like desire, is a kind of abstract negativity, while the latter involves determinate negativity.

6. Compare M109, W/C 76–7. Of course, in this regard, both the master and the slave are reinscribing the logic of desire, for which natural life of any kind was reduced to an extension of the self. In what follows, the destructive nature of the logic of desire is mediated in a crucial way by the slave's fear, its need to respect the intrinsic workings of the natural world, and by its need to transform that world into an expression of the master's will. The slave is thus put in the position to confront an expression of its own living mediation of the objective and to learn from its experience something of what it means to live as a self-consciousness. The master, whose role consists in refusing to recognize the slave's labor as an act of selfhood, and in consuming immediately its results, is only able to learn from experience its dependence on the slave. The master, in other words, continues to live in the world of desire.

7. With the notion of a "primitive" respect for the integrity of its object, I am indicating that the slave's attitude toward otherness remains within the orbit of what I have called the natural logic of consciousness. That is, its respect for the other is both exploitative and self-serving. We will see this "natural" respect repeated in the world of *Bildung*, which, in privileging the moment of singular selfhood and the need for developed selfhood, reduces its situation to expressions of utility. Only in phenomenological analysis, or induction that is fully for-itself, are the conditions for what Heidegger calls "letting-be" in place.

8. Remember that in chapter 1 I described the nature of conscious life or perception as inductive for the same reason.

9. Again, this refers us back to the distinction I made in my first chapter, between the sense in which conscious life is falsely called inductive in responding to its own posited unifying principle and inductive in responding to the demands of experience as such. The point here is that the slave is not concerned with how things appear but with *making them appear in the way they demand.* The slave's account of the natural world upon which it works is constantly under revision; the project which provides the "meaning-in-advance" shapes the world again and again, in light of the slave's increasingly adept handling. With the failure of each new initiative, the slave must be prepared to give it up and adapt its strategy, as experience prescribes.

10. Even at this point, then, prior to achieving the level of self-consciousness which greets the successful resolution of the slave's labors, we can see that he/she is engaged in precisely the kind of committed self-

evaluation or determinate negation Hegel describes in anticipating the nature of experiential development in the introduction; M79, W/C 62.

11. M 194, W/C 134.

12. That is, the principle which organizes the slave's identification of itself in its work is its own living singularity, which is precisely what was at stake in desiring self-consciousness in the previous chapter.

13. The master's embodiment in the natural world, as the principle of fear, is gradually transformed by the slave's work (in which it takes responsibility for articulating that embodiment) into the principle of singularity, the slave's life in response to fear. The abstract negativity of death, in other words, has been overcome by the assertion of finite singularity as determinate negation.

14. Remember that this was the prescription for self-consciousness, which we learned from the experience of natural or desiring self-consciousness in the last chapter.

15. In the previous chapter, above.

16. The concealment of its dependence on the institution of slavery and on the experience of consciousness will be discussed below.

17. That is, in becoming self-consciously inductive, the slave is able to become self-conscious, inductively.

18. M194, W/C 134; notice too that in M196 (W/C 135–6) Hegel argues that the slave is able to have its life as an object, only to the extent that it has identified with the fear absolutely, that is, as a self-differentiating totality.

19. In other words, the slave discovers its *living* singularity, in the terms laid down in the preceding chapter. This is the organizing insight, it seems to me, in Kojève's discussion, and it is one which he has gone to great length to elaborate. In general, Kojève's reading (with its controversial insistence on the primacy of the slave and on the confrontation or opposition between the slave and the master) is very close to my own; H. S. Harris, commenting on an earlier draft of this work, remarked that I had "out-Kojèved Kojève." It is certainly true that the argument Kojeve makes in the *Introduction à la Lecture de Hegel* has its weaknesses, but it does seem right, following Hegel, to insist on a kind of privilege being accorded the slave's experience. The slave still must gain, however, the mastery that it has given up—the story is, after all, still about "divided" selfhood at this stage—and this is the transition to stoicism. I am somewhat sympathetic with Kelly's criticism of Kojève ("Notes on Hegel's "Lordship and Bondage"") and especially with his concern to read the

Phenomenology of Spirit as a "psychology of development" (p. 196), but his insistence that there is nothing *really* social at stake here (beyond a reasonable anticipation of the chapter on reason, which he says is the first explicitly "social' section) seems to run up against Hegel's own analysis. I will return to this in my next section.

20. The term *history* carries with it here only the sense of having been worked out in time, but unified as the story of what really happened and appeared to happen in time. The relationship between the appearance of temporal succession, the inductively unifying retrospection that gathers it as history, and the concept of experience as the truth of history is the theme of section three in the next chapter.

21. Describing Hegel's notion of science, John Sallis writes:

> [s]erious otherness is no mere moment within the identity of the subject; and the overcoming of serious otherness is not to be accomplished by a mere positing of a unity correlative to such identity, by a mere positing of a unity that would immediately abolish the diversity of dismemberment. What is required is rather the toilsome gathering of diversity into unity, a gathering which, in overcoming diversity, lets it nonetheless be preserved in a new form. (p. 138)

It is in just this "toilsome gathering," the inductive self-discovery, that the experience of the slave marks the first partially explicit form of inductive science.

22. The term *institution* then names the intersubjective form of what has already arisen as the objective totality of any form of conscious life: a principled relation between an authoritative unity and the multiplicity it is said to represent.

The missing step between the intersubjective institution of slavery and the *social* institutions of Geist is reason, to which Hegel devotes his fifth chapter in the *Phenomenology of Spirit*. Although the transition is complex, I will indicate its general course. From slavery, consciousness retreats to its own singularity as stoicism. But in stoicism, it affirms the primacy of its own thoughts, which first as skepticism and then in the unhappy consciousness are taken to be what prevents and what might yet achieve (respectively) necessary and universal truths of experience.

Reason, which realizes the goal of the unhappy consciousness, is the first form of conscious life that posits the unity of the objective and the subjective, albeit according to a principle that is taken to be immediately subjective. It is precisely in the immediacy with which each and every self is supposed to recognize its own rationality, and equally to expect it from others, that the tension within reason lies. Over the course of its experience, it has to confront the fact that what is supposed to be something we already are together isn't evident in the institutions on whose terms we recognize one another. That is, the immediately inter-subjective community of rational selves has not yet actualized itself and finds instead some socially mediated artifacts governing its living reality.

Both John Russon ("Hegel's Phenomenology of Reason and Dualism") and Robert Williams (*Recognition*) provide compelling and clear accounts of the movement of the chapter as a whole and of the role of institutionalized community in particular.

23. This shows up, in the experience of the master, as the essential tension in the institution: the master's life *is* one of inflexibly prescribing how things have to be and refusing to admit that mediation in any significant way belongs to its prescriptions. The master's natural or desiring self-consciousness is still trying to learn the lesson the slave has already learned: that life, or experiencing, is a condition for selfhood.

24. My understanding of the role of the institution has been strengthened both by my reading of Russon's *Hegel on the Body* and by reading Merleau-Ponty's work on the institution as the basis for ordering and comprehending change.

25. It is crucial to any instituted slavery that the master achieve this hold over every single slave, precluding any possible sense of solidarity. Not surprisingly, such solidarity is immediately threatening to the master, because it means the slaves see themselves in one another and not in the master. The master would then cease to be the master.

26. And, as we will see, it is the relative permanence the work has for the slave that eludes the master and leaves the master with only the frustrations of desire. The master evaluates the work only by immediately consuming it, thus is deprived of the kind of experience of self-development that is open to the slave.

27. Or, in learning how to be the living means to the master's satisfaction.

28. It is important to notice that, although the history of philosophy shows us that at least some stoics had the legal status of slaves, their experience was not that of slavery. To the extent that each was capable of defining their own selfhood in singular terms, these stoics no longer

experienced the world as slaves but as singular selves trapped within an institution that no longer reflected their experience.

29. Notice that the first self has *already* been forced to respect the self-determining nature of its experience, by recognizing it as having yeilded, in the form of the other self, something threatening to its claim on selfhood.

30. M187, W/C 130–1.

31. Hegel poses this dilemma in M188 (W/C 131), but it has been evident from the outset; in turning against the conditions under which it lives, desiring self-consciousness has as its implicit model an immortal, which is to say a nonliving, or better a dead, sense of selfhood.

32. I take this to be the point to the remark Hegel makes (in M189, W/C 132) about the dissolution of the "simple unity" of selfhood posited but unfulfilled by desiring self-consciousness.

33. This is another way of affirming what we saw in the last chapter, the lesson that had to be learned by desiring self-consciousness. In recognizing its own dependence on life while awaiting recognition by another self, the struggling self-consciousness recognizes the independence of life as the object of self-consciousness.

34. M189; W/C 132: "*Bewußtsein in der Gestalt der Dingheit.*"

4. *The Experience of the Institutional Self*

1. Here again I have alluded to a stage in the development which is described at length, and in logical detail, in Hegel's chapter called "Reason." See note 22 in the previous chapter for an indication of how what the slave needs to complete its induction is furthered by reason.

2. This is the argument Hegel makes in the *Philosophy of Spirit*, when he defines the context of a nation as that stable and objectifying context of the developing realization of Spirit (pp. 277–81). In the next chapter, I will return to the connection between induction and history as it is described in the chapter called "Absolute Knowing" in the *Phenomenology of Spirit*.

A number of commentators have grappled with the explicitly historical references in the chapter called "Spirit," but few have emphasized that the experiential, "real time" development of transformation described in the chapter is, as I will argue, what defines the limitations of each of its institutions. That is, what is at stake here is the realization of an institution that knows itself as having emerged through lived transformations driven by the need to recognize the significance of lived experience itself. Terry Pinkard's chapter on "The Possibility of History" in his *Hegel's Dialectic: The Explanation of Possibility*, rightly distinguishes between Hegel's "philosophy of history—which asks how and why history is possible—and his "philosophical history." Robert Williams, in *Recognition*, makes something like the claim I am arguing for here, especially when he emphasizes, against readers like Taylor (in *Hegel and Modern Society*) that spiritual development is necessarily "empirical" (his chapter 8). At the same time, Williams wants to insist that Hegel's concern to reconcile the empirical and the transcendental is an argument *against* transcendental philosophy (pp. 193–4). In a different manner, Hyppolite argues for the necessity that Spirit be historical (*Genesis and Structure*, p. 325) but reads this in terms of Hegel's "idealism." But Hyppolite argues, as I will, that the history we are reading is driven by the need for institutional life to arrive at the recognition of its own historicality, the recognition that it has built itself from what its own experience has shown it requires.

3. While a number of commentators have identified, following Hegel, that there is a conceptual integrity at stake in the becoming concrete of social or spiritual order (among them David Kolb in *The Critique of Pure Modernity: Hegel, Heidegger, and After*, Lewis Hinchman, in *Hegel's Critique of the Enlightenment* and Terry Pinkard, in *Hegel's Dialectic: The Explanation of Possibility*), perhaps the most "Hegelian" exposition of the development of a system of recognition in terms of the destructive exclusion or isolation of singularity is John Russon's "Selfhood, Conscience, and Dialectic in Hegel's *Phenomenology of Spirit*." My analysis here follows the basic moves laid out by Russon, and I am especially grateful to have sat in on his course on Hegel when it focused on the chapter in question here. My understanding of singularity and its role in guiding the development of institutional life toward conscientious forgiveness, especially, resulted from discussions with him on these matters.

4. M444–447, W/C 291–3. We have already seen, in the last chapter, that the moment of singularity is that in which the self organizes an experienced, particular multiplicity according to some universal principle. *Sittlichkeit*, which defines the universal as immediately the truth of particular selves, has no place for singularity or for its own self-mediation.

5. M466–77, W/C 292–3. This, it seems to me, is the issue at stake in *Sittlichkeit*; a number of commentators have stated this in various ways. In its refusal to recognize selfhood outside of the selfhood of citizen-

ship and its refusal to understand its authority as flowing from the recognition of particular selves that their selfhood does depend on participation in the institution, the institution of *Sittlichkeit* replays the relation between the master and slave as the two domains of membership in one society.

6. The point here, as we will see, is that the life of *Sittlichkeit* is internally divided because of its inability to recognize the unity of its members as a dynamic, self-determining totality. Its immediate authority means it is forced to label all differences that arise within it as natural differences, or differences it is unable to mediate. When these emerge, they are immediately pitted against one another, and the community as a whole is forced to confront and give in to the conditions of its living, that is, to accept as fated the contradiction of *Sittlichkeit* as an immediate organization and as a totality mediated by its own activity.

7. The apparently natural individuality is recognized as an institution, albeit an apparent one, because to recognize any moment of selfhood at all in this stage of the development of self-consciousness is to recognize it as immediately instituted.

8. As we have seen in the analysis of *Verstand*, the concept of law depends on the law's having informed or governed the way the individual behaved and on its being the individual's *own* principle in its active singularity. To the extent that the institutions of *Sittlichkeit* deny that the individual need undertake such a self-description (it has always already done it) and that reflectively comprehending one's singularity belongs to law-governed life at all, they *understand* that membership involves singularity.

9. That is, the law which is the immediate counterpart to the self-consciously constructed human law. In light of the divisions which recur throughout *Sittlichkeit* as a result of its conscious experience of itself, the divine law is best understood as the essence of the law appropriated by this community, as authority or legality as such. The relative primacy that *Sittlichkeit ought* to accord the divine law, which represents the universal law that stands over and against the laws of the individual state as the truth they must immediately attain, is inverted because in the self-consciously ethical community the emphasis must be on the ultimacy of what it has made of the divine law in its own self-conscious legislation. (Here we see another reminder of the logic of *Verstand*, which was unable to reconcile the concept of law as such with the many determinate laws it used to understand the multiplicity of determinate appearances.) Notice, therefore, that the divine law, which represents the universal essence of legal

authority, is assigned to what is the unessential moment of the ethical community, that is, the citizen as individual, and that the human law is the essence of the ethical community or universality of selfhood. That *Sittlichkeit* tolerates and demands the realization of both laws, and that each presupposes its primacy over the other, is the self-contradiction the crisis unleashed by Antigone reveals. See M453, M456; W/C 297, 298–9.

10. Notice that, to the extent that the institution of the family is determined as significant by virtue of the division *Sittlichkeit* performs upon itself, it and the roles of its members are already *products* of the self-determining life of the community, something both the family and the nation are forced to deny.

11. We were prepared for this in our analysis of natural consciousness in chapter 2. Remember that natural consciousness can only end in death; to develop, it would have to recognize the role of life over and against its proclaimed universality as the experiential mediation of its truth. The recognition only in terms of death will turn out to be as true of membership in the state as it is of the family.

12. M452, W/C 295–7.

13. These are excluded because in each case its individuality would have to be something it *did*, which would threaten the immediacy with which individuality (in opposition both to mediating singularity and to immediate citizenship) is defined.

14. M451, W/C 294–5.

15. The family, in other words, is the institution of self-consciousness purely according to natural logic—that is, as founded on the assertion of the complete independence of the individual from both its social and its merely lived experiencing. It is the *desiring community*, where each member defines itself as the immediate truth of all the others not by outliving them and celebrating their death but by predeceasing them and achieving individuality in terms of divine law. Hegel remarks that even the act of saving a family member's life would betray, rather than express, its bond—to do so would be to attach to some contingent event, and a finite, natural life, the truth of the individual. Compare M451, W/C 294–5.

16. This is the counterpart to the death struggle which lays the ground for the emancipation of inductive, singular selfhood, and it equally lays the ground for the subsequent development of spiritual life.

17. M455, W/C 297–8.

18. *Kraft* is Hegel's term for the consciousness of the two institutions of what binds the apparent individual to the substance of the institution

and of what gets self-conscious expression in their laws (M445, W/C 291–2; M453, W/C 297). As we saw in the analysis of *Verstand*, force is what consciousness calls the dynamism it renders inert in appealing to an immediately self-identical totality of apparently real things. Miller translates *Kraft* throughout this section as "power," which captures the idea of a force determined as the individual's potential for being realized in the immediate identity of membership in the community, but which in the process conceals the continuity between the analysis of the laws of *Verstand* and the laws of *Sittlichkeit*.

19. Again, this also is an expression of the logic it shares with the relation of the master and the slave.

20. Notice here that even the calls to war, which confirm membership in the nation, and the authority of human laws, appeal to the natural authority of the divine law. See M455, W/C 297–8.

21. M463, W/C 303–4.

22. That is, the family is tolerated by the nation because in it young men are produced who represent the force that is realized in citizenship; M475, W/C 313–5.

23. The individual's act of identification with one set of laws will always appear to each institution as at best contingent and, at worst, criminally self-aggrandizing. This is because she/he could never be responsible, according to the immediate logic of *Sittlichkeit*, for choosing what she/he should already have known.

24. M468, W/C 307–9.

25. M464; W/C 304: "*[F]urchtbaren Schicksals*."

26. This is the self-consciously adopted form of what we have already seen: the institutional denial of the work of singular selves in actualizing the institution of *Sittlichkeit* was not recognized by the institution, and the experience of its members (again, like the slave) was that their truth must lie elsewhere. This now has become the principle uniting the communities we will examine in *Bildung*.

27. In this section, I am indebted to H. S. Harris' graduate seminar on the *Phenomenology of Spirit* and to John Russon's account of the logical dynamic of *Bildung* in *Hegel on the Body*, and to his graduate and undergraduate seminars on Hegel.

28. M486, W/C 321.

29. M489, W/C 324–5.

30. We will see below that one of the institutions within *Bildung*, the enlightenment, takes this view of all forms of consciousness other

than its own, *including* its counterpart, faith, in *Bildung*—that is, that it is the result of a pernicious overvaluation of determinate thoughts and an inability to see the truth of pure thinking, or reasoning. This is in part why, as Hinchman has argued (in *Hegel's Critique of the Enlightenment*), there is in the very notion of *Bildung* a constitutive claim for empiricism. I shall return to this below.

31. The primary critical weapon, and ultimately the universal self, of the enlightenment is reason. But because its universality is immediately identified with singularity, or with the work of actively reorganizing the world according to the power of reason, it is appropriate to characterize membership in the enlightenment as an identity with reason*ing*.

32. In many respects, the self's relation to its determinate circumstances or situation, from the standpoint of *Bildung*, has the force of a *denunciation* of what Heidegger calls "*die Geworfenheit*," or the *thrownness*, of finite existing selfhood. That is, the self in *Bildung* always looks on the determinate structure or order of meaning, value, significance, as an alien and limiting being over and against its true potential. Finding oneself in this or that situation is always an accident of nature and an accident that needs to be corrected.

33. The destructive moment of the terror follows upon the recognition that no positive work could be undertaken, precisely because it would mean my making this difference here, on behalf of universal singularity; the standard is such that anything I do results in the same compromise that exists as the call to universal action. This is the argument in paragraphs M586–8, W/C 388–9.

34. M487, W/C 323; M489, W/C 324–5.

35. That faith identifies as its pure self a "pure *consciousness*" (M487, W/C 323) indicates that for faith, God is something otherworldly, something over and against the natural world. That is, God is determinate, determined by the opposition to this world. This is the difference between the worlds of faith and manifest religion, for which God is reconciled with this world. Quentin Lauer captures the flight from actuality very well in A *Reading of Hegel's Phenomenology of Spirit* (pp. 199–211), as does Kojève, who rightly notes the double aspect of *Bildung*: as self-formation, it must equally be the transformation of the actual world, and the denial of the latter condemns the former to fail (*Introduction à la Lecture de Hegel*, pp. 179–80).

36. M541–2, W/C 357–8.

37. M541, W/C 357.

38. Lewis Hinchman, in the third chapter of *Hegel's Critique of the Enlightenment*, compares the discussions of rationalist metaphysics and empiricism from the *Encyclopedia Logic* with *Bildung* to draw out the importance of the philosophical movements of the historical Enlightenment in articulating its central attitudes.

39. Compare M167, W/C 120–22.

40. Remember that it was the emergence of another self-consciousness, and the ensuing death struggle, that forced desire to come to recognize the need, not only for a developed relationship to its experiencing but also for a consensual approach to selfhood.

41. It is in this separation that the world of revolution and terror is equally the world of the "birth" of the material sciences; M576–8, W/C 380–2.

42. M557, W/C 368–9.

43. M553, W/C 365. Of course, it is regressive only to the extent that the development of self-consciousness sharpens the same emphasis on selfhood that consciousness sharpened in terms of the objective sphere; just as consciousness had to become "subjective," self-consciousness needs to become "objective." The crisis of the terror is the result of its inability to do just that, thus it is the final stage in preparing self-consciousness to recognize the need to become objective, to lay claim on things.

44. M558, W/C 369–70.

45. Hinchman connects this aspect of Enlightenment empiricism to Locke and draws on Hegel's lectures on Locke to fill out the basis of the analysis I will pursue here. Hinchman also makes the connection I have been making to *Verstand*, which resurfaces in sublated form throughout the analysis of *Bildung*. Hyppolite also conveys the sense in which the Enlightenment's return to sensuous certainty marks the triumph of reasoning or intellection itself as the freedom of a thought liberated from traditional categories (*Genesis and Structure*, pp. 444–5). Something very much like Hegel's analysis here occurs in section 20 of *Being and Time*, in Heidegger's criticism of the Cartesian model of worldhood and its fascination with material nature.

46. M588, 388–9.

47. M635, W/C 417–8.

48. M642: "Insofar as this knowing has in it the moment of *universality*, conscientious action requires that the actual case before it should be viewed unrestrictedly in all its bearings and therefore that all of the cir-

cumstances of the case should be accurately known and taken into consideration." W/C 422: "*Insofern das Moment der Allgemeinheit an diesem Wissen ist, gehört zum Wissen des gewissenhaften Handelns, die vorliegende Wirklichkeit auf uneingeschränkte Weise zu umfassen, und also die Umstände des Falles genau zu wissen und in Erwägung zu ziehen.*"

49. M640, W/C 420–1; M647, W/C 426.

50. And, equally important, it has realized the goal of morality: to submit its actions to the authority of universal selfhood. The crucial difference, of course, is that the universal selfhood is what it shares with others as the living institutional context. Compare M606, W/C 401.

51. M639–40, W/C 419–21.

52. M642, W/C 422.

53. M642; W/C 422: "*Eine absolute Vielheit der Umstände, die sich rückwärts in ihre Bedingungen, seitwärts in ihrem Nebeneinander, vorwärts in ihren Folgen unendlich teilt und ausbreitet.*" I am grateful to John Russon for calling this passage to my attention.

Remember that in sensuous certainty, the singular now found its truth as one of an "absolute plurality" of nows. With conscience that finds its singular self expressed in a plurality of its own determinations, we have returned to the reflective ideal of immediacy as a product of the labor of experiencing consciousness.

54. M642, W/C 422.

55. The necessity of forgiveness is posited, as I suggest, in the very limits of the act of conviction; but it is only in the culminating moments of the experience of the institution of conscience that forgiveness resolves the conflict between the knowledge of the context that universality ought to have and the situated, motivated, *interested* singularity that has to act. Compare M670, W/C 440–1. John Russon's "Conscience, Selfhood, and Dialectic in Hegel's *Phenomenology of Spirit*" provides a detailed account of the role of forgiveness in completing the logic of conscience and of that completion as the culmination of the project of becoming a self in phenomenological terms.

5. *Induction and the Experience of Phenomenology*

1. M792, W/C 518–9.

2. M797, W/C 522. This explains the relative primacy assigned the moment of conscience and forgiveness over the realization of the institution of conscience in the form of the religious community. The commu-

nity of manifest religion (I take the term *manifest* from H. S. Harris' graduate seminar on the *Phenomenology of Spirit*) is the community that has given itself the language which is appropriated in the expression of conviction and which has equally given itself the language with which to forgive those acts. In other words, it knows itself to be responsible for the forms singular conviction takes, thus it is the necessary condition for forgiveness. The act of singular selfhood as forgiving, which has the being of the religious community as its integrated object, or for-itself, is the completion of the education of experiencing singularity which we began in sensuous certainty.

3. Again, as John Sallis argues (in "Hegel's Concept of Presentation"), "it does not *impose* this unity upon the diversity that reigns among and within the shapes of spirit . . . it *holds out* this unity to the shapes, *lets* them develop into it, that is, lets them show themselves as already self-gathered into such a unity" (p. 156).

4. Compare M89, W/C 68.

5. M797, W/C 522: "*die Versammlung*." The act of forgiveness is realized as the phenomenological system of experiencing, or the phenomenology of phenomenology, the gathered forms of convinced singularity that we have described.

The term *gathering*, which John Sallis uses repeatedly, is Heidegger's translation of *logos* in his "The Being and Conception of *Phusis* in Aristotle's *Physics*, B, I."

6. M26, W/C 19–21, describes the need for science to show itself as already animating the behavior of natural singularity and the phenomenological analysis shows just that in organizing the systematic expression of the moments of the concept of experience. See also M53, W/C 39–40.

7. M801, W/C 524–5.

8. M798, W/C 523. This is distinct from the religious community, which tolerates and forgives the manifold expressions of singularity abstractly by absolving them of their determinateness. Again, the notion of being "one of God's creatures," in its abstractness, seems to call for death as the realization of the community singular religious selves.

9. Remember that in my account of what desire had yet to accomplish, I argued that it required the experiencing it called itself the truth of to recognize it truth on its own; in the phenomenological act of forgiveness, this means showing how each form of experiencing consciousness calls for phenomenology, that is, how it shows itself to require phenomenology to tell its own story.

10. M800; W/C 523–4: "*[Als der Geist] existiert er früher nicht, und sonst nirgends als nach Vollendung der Arbeit, seine unvollkommene Gestaltung zu bezwingen, sich für sein Bewußtsein die Gestalt seines Wesens zu vershaffen, und auf diese Weise sein Selbstbewußtsein mit seinem Bewußtsein auszugleichen.*"

11. Of course, we have known that the shapes of experiencing were temporally prior to the self-comprehension of experiencing as phenomenology, or induction that is in-and-for-itself, since our analysis of desiring self-consciousness showed us that desire had to learn from its objects what its truth was. It depends on them to show it how to comprehend them. That is why it has to learn to be *inductive*—it has to learn from experience what experiencing is.

We have known since our analysis of everyday consciousness, or perception, that experiencing as such was prior to any shape, but only as what Hegel calls substance. Its prior presence shows up as what conditions the form of truth recognized in perception.

12. There is a sense in which the inductive development on which it depends is what makes the science sensitive to the need to provide other forms of natural singularity with the "ladder": that is, the inductive development itself and what enables it to carry this out within its own scientific, or deductive, form. See M26, W/C 19–21.

13. Again, we have seen how both desiring self-consciousness and *Bildung* turn what we know to be a history of experiencing consciousness into food—that is, into something to be consumed without recognizing the role of time. The slave, on the other hand, wins back its sense of self from time, as the measure of the experience it has learned from. The slave is perhaps the only shape of conscious life prior to conscience for which time means anything other than the measure of self-refutation, or the sign of its mortality, or death.

14. I take this to be the sense of Hegel's remark in M801, W/C 524–5, that time is grasped by consciousness as "empty intuition" ("*leere Anschauung*"). The point is that time serves consciousness as a backup or default mode in the event of a crisis or breakdown in its principled claim to know what is going on in experience.

15. This is what I analyzed in the first chapter as "determinate negation."

16. One of the clearest explications of the relationship between history and knowledge in Hegel's philosophy is A. Robert Caponigri's "The Pilgrimage of Truth Through Time: The Conception of the History of

Philosophy in G. W. F. Hegel." Stepping back from his specific topic, Caponigri suggests that historicity as a category in Hegelian philosophy is opposed to temporality as a *contretemps*, as the act of taking back from time what belongs to selfhood. Nonetheless, time "is an absolute ingredient of the Idea." This captures well not only the argument I am focusing on here but also the fundamental tension that pulls the intellectual practice of historiography apart—its commitment to giving to time with one hand the responsibility for ordering its object, and snatching it back through concepts which provide their own order with the other.

17. From volume one of *Capital*. Marx is very rigid in his insistence on a similar kind of inductive method and historical respect for inductive development, although a number of critics accuse him, as he accused Hegel, of abstract and presupposed concepts. An excellent defense of the side of Marx that I am calling inductive can be found in Derek Sayer's work *The Violence of Abstraction*.

18. M802; W/C 525: "*daß nichts gewußt wird, was nicht in der Erfahrung ist*."

19. M802, W/C 525–6; M803, W/C 526–7.

20. M803, W/C 526–7.

21. M802, W/C 525–6.

22. M807, W/C 529–30. Hegel writes, recalling what we learned of death and sacrifice in the analysis of desire, that "to know one's limit is to know how to sacrifice oneself" ("*[s]eine Grenze wissen, heißt sich aufzuopfern wissen*").

23. I have argued, following Hegel's account of experiencing, that induction is the method, but only in phenomenology, or induction in- and for-itself, do we learn why.

24. Thereby fulfilling the promise made in the analysis of desire, that self-consciousness would have to "learn through experience that the object is independent"; M168, W/C 168.

25. *Science of Logic* 28.

26. It seems, then, that the science of these "pure essentialities" will have little in common with the science of experiencing, at least insofar as the role of induction is concerned: we know now what science is and how to proceed scientifically.

27. It is this sense of preparation that Hegel alludes to in the introduction to the *Philosophy of Right* stating that the concept of right, or at least its deduction, is presupposed by that work, a remark similar to the one made in the introduction to the *Science of Logic*.

28. This continuity is clearest in the opening sections of the course, in which Hegel defends the striking notion that philosophy has and must have a history. In keeping with the notion of inductive development, he contrasts a history of necessary and explicit stages of development with one in which the logic that is developing remains concealed in each of the stages, which then lack expressed continuity. Again, in such a case, we historians can see that necessity tacitly working itself out in "the empirical form" (*LHP* p. 30).

Bibliography

Primary Texts, in German

Hegel, G. W. F., *Erste Drückschriften*, hrsg. von Georg Lasson, Leipzig: Felix Meiner Verlag, 1928.

———. *Phänomenologie des Geistes*, hrsg. von Hans-Friedrich Wessels und Heinrich Clairmont, Hamburg: Felix Meiner Verlag, 1988.

———. *Vorlesungen über die Geschichte der Philosophie III*, Band 20, Franfurt am Main: Suhrkamp Verlag, 1971.

———. *Vorlesungen über die Philosophie der Geschichte*, Band 12, Frankfurt am Main: Suhrkamp Verlag, 1970.

———. *Wissenschaft der Logik*, hrsg. von Georg Lasson, Hamburg: Felix Meiner Verlag, 1967.

English Translations

———. *Lectures on the History of Philosophy*, trans. E. S. Haldane and Frances H. Simson, New York: The Humanities Press, 1974.

———. *The Encyclopedia Logic*, trans. T.F. Geraets, W.A. Suchting, H.S. Harris; Indianapolis: Hackett Publishing Company, 1991.

———. *Phenomenology of Spirit*, trans. A.V. Miller, Oxford: Oxford University Press, 1977.

———. *Philosophy of History*, trans. J. Sibree, New York: Dover, 1956.

———. *Philosophy of Mind, Being Part Three of the Encyclopedia of the Philosophical Sciences*, trans. William Wallace and A.V. Miller, Oxford: Clarendon Press, 1971.

———. *Philosophy of Right*, trans. T. M. Know, Oxford: Oxford University Press, 1967.

———. "Relationship of Skepticism to Philosophy, Exposition of Its Different Modifications and Comparison to the Latest Form with the Ancient One," trans. H. S. Harris, in di Giovanni and Harris (eds.) *Between Kant and Hegel: Texts in the Development of Post-Kantian Idealism*, Albany: State University of New York Press, 1985.

———. *Science of Logic*, trans. A.V. Miller, New York: Humanities Press, 1976.

Readings of Hegel

Adorno, Theodor, "*Erfahrungsgehalt*," in *Drei Studien zu Hegel*, Frankfurt am Main: Suhrkamp Verlag, 1971, pp. 53–83.

Bataille, Georges, "Hegel, Death and Sacrifice," *Yale French Studies*, 78 (1990), pp. 9–28.

Baur, Michael, "Hegel and the Overcoming of the Understanding," *Owl of Minerva*, 22, 2, 1991, pp. 141–58.

Berthold-Bond, Daniel, "Hegel's Eschatological Vision: Does History Have a Future?," *History and Theory*, 27, 1988, pp. 14–29.

Caponigri, A. Robert, "The Pilgrimage of Truth Through Time: The Conception of the History of Philosophy in G. W. F. Hegel," in O'Malley, Algozin, and Weiss (eds.) *Hegel and the History of Philosophy*, pp. 1–20.

De Nys, Martin J., "Force and the Understanding: The Unity of the Object of Consciousness," in Westphal (eds.), *Method and Speculation in Hegel's Phenomenology*, pp. 57–70.

———. "Self-Consciousness and the Concept in Hegel's Appropriation of Kant," in Ardis B. Collins (ed.) *Hegel on the Modern World*, Albany: State University of New York Press, 1995, pp. 143–58.

Dove, Kenley Royce, "Hegel's 'Deduction of the Concept,'" in Cohen and Wartofsky (eds.) *Hegel and the Sciences*, Boston: Kluwer Academic Publishers, pp. 271–81.

———. “Hegel's Phenomenological Method,” *Review of Metaphysics*, 23, 1970, pp. 613–41.

———. “Phenomenology and Systematic Philosophy,” in Westphal (ed.) *Method and Speculation in Hegel's Phenomenology*, pp. 27–39.

Findlay, J. N., *Hegel: A Re-examination*, London: George Allen and Unwin, 1958.

Flay, Joseph P., *Hegel's Quest for Certainty*, Albany: State University of New York Press, 1984.

———. “Hegel's Inverted World,” *Review of Metaphysics*, 23, 1970, pp. 662–78.

———. “Pragmatic Presuppositions and the Dialectics of Hegel's Phenomenology,” in Westphal (ed.), *Method and Speculation in Hegel's Phenomenology*, pp. 15–26.

Gadamer, Hans Georg, *Hegel's Dialectic: Five Hermeneutical Studies*, trans. P. Christopher Smith, New Haven: Yale University Press, 1976.

Harris, Errol E., “Dialectic and Scientific Method,” *Idealistic Studies*, 3, 1973, pp. 1–17.

Harris, H. S., “Comment on Phenomenology As Systematic Philosophy,” in Westphal (ed.) *Method and Speculation in Hegel's Phenomenology*, pp. 41–6.

Heidegger, Martin, “*Hegel's Begriff der Erfahrung*,” in *Holzwege*, Frankfurt am main: Klostermann, 1950.

Hinchman, Lewis P., *Hegel's Critique of the Enlightenment*, University Presses of Florida, 1984.

Houlgate, Stephen, *Hegel, Nietzsche, and the Criticism of Metaphysics*, Cambridge: Cambridge University Press, 1986.

Hyppolite, Jean, *Genesis and Structure of Hegel's Phenomenology of Spirit*, trans. Samuel Cherniak and John Heckman, Evanston: Northwestern University Press, 1974.

Kainz, Howard P., *Hegel's Phenomenology Part I: Analysis and Commentary*, University of Alabama Press, 1976.

Kojève, Alexandre, *Introduction à la Lecture de Hegel*, Gallimard, 1947.

Lampert, Jay, “Husserl and Hegel on the Logic of Subjectivity,” *Man and World*, 21, 1988, pp. 363–93.

Lauer, Quentin, S. J., *A Reading of Hegel's Phenomenology of Spirit*, New York: Fordham University Press, 1976.

Levin, David Michael, “Induction and Husserl's Theory of Eidetic

Variation," *Philosophy and Phenomenological Research*, 29, 1968, pp. 1–15.

Marcuse, Herbert, *Hegel's Ontology and the Theory of Historicity*, trans. Seyla Benhabib, Cambridge: The MIT Press, 1987.

Marx, Werner, *Hegel's Phenomenology of Spirit*, trans. Peter Heath, Chicago: University of Chicago Press, 1975.

McCumber, John, *The Company of Words. Hegel, Language, and Systematic Philosophy*, Evanston: Northwestern University Press, 1993.

Pinkard, Terry, *Hegel's Dialectic: The Explanation of Possibility*, Philadelphia: Temple University Press, 1988.

Pippin, Robert, *Hegel's Idealism. The Satisfactions of Self-Consciousness*, Cambridge: Cambridge University Press, 1989.

———. "You Can't Get There From Here: Transition Problems in Hegel's *Phenomenology of Spirit*, in Frederick C. Beiser (ed.) *The Cambridge Companion to Hegel*, Cambridge: Cambridge University Press, 1993, pp. 52–85.

———. "Hegel's Phenomenological Criticism," in *Man and World*, vol. 8, #3, August 1975, pp. 296–314.

Preuss, Peter, "Selfhood and the Battle: The Second Beginning of the *Phenomenology*," in Westphal (ed.) *Method and Speculation in Hegel's Phenomenology*, pp. 71–83.

Rosenthal, Abigail L., "A Hegelian Key to Hegel's Method," *Journal of the History of Philosophy*, 9, 1971, pp. 205–12.

Russon, John, "Hegel's `Freedom of Self-Consciousness' and Early Modern Epistemology," in *Hegel and the Tradition: Essays in Honor of H. S. Harris* (University of Toronto Press, forthcoming).

———. "Selfhood, Conscience, and Dialectic in Hegel's *Phenomenology of Spirit*," *Southern Journal of Philosophy*, XXIX, 4, 1991, pp. 533–50.

———. "Reading and the Body in Hegel," in *Clio*, 22:4, 1993, pp. 321–36.

———. "Hegel's Phenomenology of Reason and Dualism," in *Southern Journal of Philosophy*, XXXI, 1, 1993, pp. 71–96.

———. *Hegel on the Body*, doctoral dissertation, University of Toronto, 1990.

Sallis, John, "Hegel's Concept of Presentation," *Hegel-Studien*, 12, 1977, pp. 129–56.

Schmitz, Kenneth L., "Hegel on Kant: Being-in-Itself and the Thing-in-Itself," in Kennington (ed.), *Studies in Philosophy and the History* of *Philosophy*, vol. 12, Washington, D. C.: Catholic University of America Press, 1985, pp. 229–51.

Schrader, George, "Hegel's Contribution to Phenomenology," *Monist*, 48, 1, 1964, pp. 18–33.

Solomon, Robert C., "Hegel's Concept of *Geist*," in *From Hegel to Existentialism*, Oxford: Oxford University Press, 1987.

Suchting, W. A., "Hegel and the Humean Problem of Induction," in *Studies in the History and Philosophy of Science*, vol. 21, #3, 1990, pp. 493–510.

Taylor, Charles, *Hegel and the Modern State*, Cambridge: Cambridge University Press, 1979.

———. "The Opening Arguments of the *Phenomenology*," in MacIntyre (ed.), *Hegel: a Collection of Critical Essays*, Notre Dame: University of Notre Dame Press, 1976, pp. 151–87.

Thagard, Paul, "Hegel, Science, and Set Theory," *Erkenntnis*, 18, 1982, pp. 397–410.

Warminski, Andrej, *Readings in Interpretation*, Minneapolis: University of Minnesota Press, 1987.

Williams, Robert B., *Recognition: Fichte and Hegel on the Other*, Albany: State University of New York Press, 1992.

Other Works

Aristotle, *Posterior Analytics*, trans. G. R. G. Mure, in *The Basic Works of Aristotle*, Richard McKeon, (ed.), New York: Random House, 1941.

Bateson, Gregory, *Steps to an Ecology of Mind*, Toronto: Chandler Publishing Company, 1972.

Bertoldi, Eugene, "Phenomenology of Phenomenology," *Canadian Journal of Philosophy*, VII, 2, 1977, pp. 239–53.

Black, Max, *Language and Philosophy*, Ithaca: Cornell University Press, 1949.

Collingwood, R. G. *Speculum Mentis*, Oxford: Clarendon Press, 1946.

Dewey, John, *Experience and Nature*, Carbondale: Southern Illinois University Press, 1988.

Goodman, Nelson, *Fact, Fiction, and Forecast*, Cambridge: Harvard University Press, 1983, 4th ed.

Heidegger, Martin, "On the Being and Conception of *Phusis* in Aristotle's *Physics* B, I," *Man and World*, 9, 1976, pp. 219–70.

———. *Being and Time*, trans. John Macquarrie and Edward Robinson, New York: Harper and Row, 1962.

Hume, David, *A Treatise of Human Nature*, L. A. Selby-Bigge (ed.), Oxford: Clarendon Press, 1951.

Kant, Immanuel, *Critique of Pure Reason*, trans. Norman Kemp Smith, London: Macmillan and Company, 1961.

Katz, Jerrold J., *The Problem of Induction and Its Solution*, Chicago: University of Chicago Press, 1962.

Kosman, L. A., "Understanding, Explanation, and Insight in Aristotle's *Posterior Analytics*," in E. N. Lee, A. P. D. Mourelatos, R. M. Rorty (eds.) *Exegesis and Argument*, Assen: Van Gorcum and Company, 1973.

Marx, Karl, *Capital, Volume One*, trans. Ben Fowkes, New York: Vintage Books, 1977.

Merleau-Ponty, Maurice, *Phenomenology of Perception*, trans. Colin Smith, London: Routledge and Kegan Paul, 1962.

Mill, John Stuart, *A System of Logic*, Charlottesville: Ibis Publishing (an undated facsimile of the Harper and Brothers edition of 1874).

Reichenbach, Hans, *The Rise of Scientific Philosophy*, Berkeley and Los Angeles: University of California Press, 1951.

Russell, Bertrand, *Problems of Philosophy*, London: Oxford University Press, 1976.

Russon, John, "Self-Consciousness and the Tradition in Aristotle's Psychology," (unpublished).

Salmon, Wesley C., *Logic*, Englewood Cliffs: Prentice-Hall, 1963.

Skyrms, Brian, *Choice and Chance: An Introduction to Inductive Logic*, 3rd ed., Belmont: Wadsworth Publishing Company, 1986.

Name Index

Author's Note: The primary purpose of an index is to provide a supplement to the table of contents. If the latter is a more generalized route map through the text, the index is a map of specific locations through which one passes on the way. In this sense, the index is more 'democratic' than the table of contents; it allows the reader to pick and choose where he or she joins the journey, and when to leave. This index is by such a description somewhat 'autocratic', and the reader deserves an explanation.

First, the text is written in a manner that parallels Hegel's text, and since it is of interest to readers of Hegel's work, it is assumed that the reader will be familiar with the shapes of conscious life which serve as the organizing principles of the various chapters, and so able to locate with relative ease discussions that are of interest. Second, the themes which I introduce in reading Hegel's text are named and developed at almost every turn, and so indexing concepts like "experience" or "induction" would lead to page references to almost the entire text. Dividing these lengthy references up by sub-themes would lead to regrouping the references by chapters, a service already provided by the table of contents. For these reasons (and also in part because of the brevity of the text) I have chosen to index the names of philosophers familiar to readers whose place in the text is not evident from the table of contents.